GRILL AND WAFFLE COOKBOOK

G R I L L *and*

cookbook

GRAMERCY PUBLISHING COMPANY

NEW YORK

WAFFLE

by *Helen S. Hovey and Roslyn W. Chidekel*

ILLUSTRATED BY NATHAN GLUCK

Dedicated to William Chidekel and Charles Hovey, our taste testers par excellence, in appreciation for their enthusiasm and assistance.

contents

GRILL AND WAFFLE COOKBOOK

1 *how to enjoy your grill and waffle baker*

All over the country—at dining tables, in pint-size apartments, suburban rumpus rooms, summer cottages or trailers, and most often at kitchen counters—the grill and waffler is a happy addition to good living. Most popular of all cooking appliances, (an estimated 14,789,000 were in use in January 1955) the combination grill and waffle baker serves many useful functions. It grills, toasts, pan-broils, fries, sautés, bakes and heats. This 7-star performer prepares eye-opening breakfasts, satisfying luncheons, party treats, and meals for expected and unexpected guests.

The *grill* is a wide flat surface used for toasting sandwiches, pan-broiling meats, and sautéing many other foods. When used for pancakes, plain and French toast, and scrambling eggs, the flat surface is referred to as a *griddle*. Aluminum *grids* are for baking waffles. The appliances are available in many different makes and several styles. You may buy a waffler, a grill, or a combination of both. If you are trying to decide which one to get, we do recommend the combination as the most useful. Look for grids which are deep and narrow, if you like especially crisp waffles. If you already own a grill or waffler but are not getting the most from it, we hope this book will show you new ways to use it every day in convenient table-top cooking.

EASY TO USE

Just plug it into a wall socket. No additional wiring is needed. Only minimum space is required on a work surface or table, so keep the grill handy for quick use. It will help make a dull meal exciting! Each appliance is accompanied by a small book of instructions. Directions for different makes are similar. In automatic models, the dial for temperature control regulates heat for every cooking need. In non-automatic models, experiment a bit until you become familiar with special features, just as you develop skill in handling a sewing machine, chafing dish, or other modern home-making appliance.

SEASONING THE WAFFLE BAKER

Many grids are already seasoned, and manufacturer's directions will indicate this. Generally, if seasoning is necessary, brush both grids, upper and lower, with salad oil or melted, unsalted shortening. Close the waffle baker, and heat at highest temperature until the signal light goes out, about 8 minutes. Unless the seasoning is washed off or the grids burn, it will not be necessary to season them again.

PREHEATING

When preparing the grill for use, preheat it closed, as heating a closed grill is much faster. Always close the waffle baker before preheating. Follow the manufacturer's directions as to time . . . generally, preheat for about 8 minutes.

CLEANING

Appliances should be left open after use, to make cleaning easier. Otherwise food particles will be burned onto the grill by retained heat. Let the grill-waffler cool before attempting to clean. Clean the grill or griddle with a paper towel or cloth dipped in warm suds, or brush gently with a pad of fine steel wool. Do not wash the waffle baker grids. Clean them with a stiff brush and a damp cloth if food particles adhere. Waffle grids become darkened with use. This is to be expected. Do not clean darkened waffle grids, unless particles of batter have burned on. If grids are washed, season them again according to the directions earlier in this chapter. If the exterior chrome finish becomes dull or stains from an overflow of food, clean it with a damp cloth and occasionally with silver polish to restore its high luster. With minimum care the appliance should be kept shining bright and attractive—ever ready to perform in a matter of minutes.

SO INEXPENSIVE

The grill-waffle baker is inexpensive to purchase and costs only a few cents a day to operate. Sturdy construction generally keeps repairs and maintenance at a mininum. The grill and cast aluminum grids will last indefinitely. As a matter of fact, in the family of one of the authors of this book is a waffler which is 25 years old, and has never once required repairs although it is in almost continual use! So if you divide the purchase price of the many number of years the appliance will last, you will see why it is one of the least expensive additions to your cooking pleasure and convenience.

2 *table-made canapés, appetizers and party snacks*

Informal entertaining should be fun, easy on the hostess, and done with a certain flair. It may be a spur-of-the-moment party, or one planned days in advance, but the food must be attractive and interesting enough to stimulate the appetite.

The simplest canapés and tidbits, served on heated crackers or toast made on a table grill, are a satisfying accompaniment for fruit and vegetable juices . . . even for stronger beverages! Toppings of meat, fish, cheese and egg may be prepared and refrigerated for use when needed. Hot appetizers such as kabobs and miniature hamburgers may be done early in the day and grilled at the last minute. Be sure these little finger foods are firm enough to be impaled on a toothpick or skewer and at the same time zesty enough to be inviting.

If you are a hostess busy with other details of the meal, appoint an amateur chef who will welcome the opportunity of handling a grill before an audience. Every crowd has one or more uninhibited souls who will be delighted to perform. With a grill on the table, guests are in on the fun of cooking and eating . . . and even the hostess can relax!

COCKTAIL KABOBS

6 cocktail sausages, cut in ½ inch cubes

3 dill pickles, cut in ½ inch cubes

20 mushroom caps

3 tablespoons French dressing

Preheat grill to 3 or M. String sausages, pickles and mushrooms alternately on 3-inch metal skewers or toothpicks. Brush lightly with French dressing. Place skewers on preheated open grill for 2 minutes or until hot, turn to grill other side. Serve hot.

HAM AND PINEAPPLE KABOBS. Alternate ½ inch cubes of ham, ham loaf, or Canadian bacon and pineapple wedges, on 3-inch metal skewers. Place skewers on preheated open grill for 2 minutes or until hot. Turn to grill other side. Serve hot.

SHISH KABOBS. Alternate ¾ inch cubes lean lamb, button mushrooms, and cocktail onions wrapped in ½ slices of bacon, on 3-inch metal skewers. Place skewers on preheated open grill for 5 minutes or until cooked. Turn to grill other side. Serve hot.

MIXED SEAFOOD KABOBS. Alternate bay or sea scallops or shrimp, mushroom caps or cocktail onions on 3-inch metal skewers. Marinate for 15 minutes in French dressing. Place skewers on preheated open grill for 5 minutes or until cooked. Turn to grill other side. Serve hot.

PARMESAN TRIANGLES
16-24 servings

¾ cup grated Parmesan cheese
⅓ cup cream
2 tablespoons chopped parsley

2 tablespoons chopped pimiento
8 slices white bread
⅓ cup chopped nuts

Preheat grill at 3 or M. Combine and mix well cheese, cream, parsley, and pimiento. Remove crusts from bread and cut slices into triangles. Spread cheese mixture on bread. Top with chopped nuts. Brown on preheated open grill for 2 minutes. Serve hot.

CHEESE PUFFS

1 egg white
¼ cup salad dressing
2 tablespoons grated sharp cheese

⅛ teaspoon dry mustard
Sprinkle of cayenne
Crackers

Preheat grill at 3 or M. Beat egg white until stiff. Fold in salad dressing, cheese, mustard and cayenne. Spread on crackers. Brown on preheated open grill for 1 minute. Serve hot.

GRILLED MUSHROOMS
24 filled mushrooms

24 mushrooms
Melted butter or margarine
½ cup filling: minced cooked

Ham or crabmeat, or sharp cheese

Preheat grill at 3 or M. Wipe mushrooms with a damp cloth. Remove stems and reserve for gravy or soups. Brush mushroom caps with melted butter. Brush grill with melted butter. Heat mushroom caps on grill, cup side down, for 3 minutes. Remove from grill, fill with desired stuffing and return to grill to heat for 2 minutes. Serve hot.

BACON BITES
24 bites

12 slices bacon, cut in half 12 stuffed olives
6 cocktail sausages, cut in half

Preheat grill at 3 or M. Roll a bacon slice around each sausage half and stuffed olive. Fasten with a toothpick. Brown on pre-heated open grill for 2 minutes or until bacon is well done, turning once. Serve hot on toothpick.

Note: Cooked shrimp, dates stuffed with cheese, cooked artichoke hearts, pickle slices, pineapple chunks, cubes of sharp cheese or ham, cocktail onions or any filling which is cooked or does not require cooking may be used successfully.

COCKTAIL MEAT BITES
18 miniature hamburgers

½ pound ground meat 1 teaspoon minced onion
2 tablespoons fine crumbs Salt and pepper to taste
2 tablespoons milk ¼ cup all-purpose flour
1 egg, slightly beaten Melted fat
2 tablespoons melted fat

Preheat grill at 3 or M. Combine and mix well: meat, crumbs, milk, egg, melted fat, onion, salt and pepper. Shape into balls the size of marbles. Roll in flour. Brush grill with melted fat. Brown meat balls on preheated open grill. Turn to grill other side. Serve on toothpicks. Use a sharp tomato sauce dip if desired. Serve hot.

To avoid last minute rushes, prepare appetizers such as Bacon Bites and Cocktail Meat Bites several hours in advance and re-frigerate. Grill when and as needed.

WAFFLED CANAPÉS
8 canapés

4 slices thin bread	2 tablespoons butter
2 slices boiled ham	½ teaspoon horseradish, if
2 slices Swiss cheese	desired

Preheat waffle baker at 3 or M. Remove crusts from sliced bread. Cut ham and cheese to fit bread. Spread bread with butter and horseradish. Place cheese and ham between slices. Cut into quarters and place in preheated waffle baker for 1 minute or until golden brown. Serve hot.

CHICKEN LIVER CRISPIES
12 crispies

¾ cup cooked chicken livers, chopped	1 teaspoon lemon juice
	½ teaspoon salt
2 tablespoons minced cooked bacon	12 crackers or toast squares (page 75)
1 teaspoon minced onion	

Preheat grill at 3 or M. Combine and mix well livers, bacon, onion, lemon juice and salt. Spread on crackers or toast. Brown on preheated open grill for 1 minute. Serve hot.

HOW TO GRILL FROZEN TIDBITS

Frozen fish sticks	Frozen codfish balls
Frozen ham sticks	Canned tamales, drained

Preheat grill at 3 or M. Cut defrosted appetizers into 1-inch sections. Brown both sides for 5 to 10 minutes on an open grill. Serve on toothpicks. A sharp tomato sauce dip adds interest. Tartar sauce is popular with fish appetizers. Serve hot.

SNAPPY SARDINE CANAPÉS
15 canapés

1 can (3¼ ounces) sardines	5 slices white bread
¼ cup grated Parmesan cheese	Prepared mustard

Preheat grill at 3 or M. Drain sardines, roll in grated cheese and reserve. Remove crusts from bread and cut each slice into thirds. Brush bread strips lightly with mustard. Place a sardine on each strip. Heat on a preheated open grill for 2 minutes. Serve immediately.

SPICY COCKTAIL SHRIMP
24 canapés

24 medium shrimp	2 tablespoons chopped parsley
¼ cup salad oil	½ teaspoon dry mustard
juice of ½ lemon	½ teaspoon salt
½ clove garlic, minced	

Preheat grill at 3 or M. Prepare shrimp by removing dark vein. Combine and mix oil, lemon juice, garlic, parsley, mustard and salt. Toss shrimp in this mixture and allow to remain for 1 hour. Place on preheated open grill for 4 minutes or until shrimp are pink; turn to grill other side. Serve on toothpicks immediately.

SURPRISE ROLLS
24 rolls

12 slices boiled ham, cut in half	8 melon or pickle fingers
8 cooked asparagus spears	Melted butter or margarine
8 cheese strips	

Preheat grill at 3 or M. Place one asparagus, cheese or melon finger on each ham slice. Roll. Fasten with toothpicks. Brush preheated grill with melted butter. Place rolls on open grill to heat and brown slightly. Serve hot.

RUSSIAN BLINI—AMERICAN VERSION
12 blini

12 3-inch buckwheat pancakes (Recipe page 82)	Sour cream
Melted butter or margarine	Caviar, smoked salmon, or cottage cheese

Preheat grill at 3 or M. Prepare buckwheat pancakes as directed. Butter and stack them. Top with sour cream. Serve hot with caviar, sliced smoked salmon, or cottage cheese.

an appetizing pizza in less than 10 minutes

QUICK PIZZA—AMERICAN STYLE
8 small pizzas

4 English muffins	Garlic salt to taste
8 slices Mozzarella cheese, or mild American	Oregano to taste
½ cup tomato sauce	Grated Parmesan cheese
½ cup salad oil	Anchovies, optional
	Sliced olives, optional

1   Turn dial to 3 or M and preheat grill.
2   Split muffins in half. Toast cut-side down on preheated grill.
3   On each toasted side place a slice of cheese. Sprinkle with 1 tablespoon tomato sauce, 1 tablespoon salad oil, a dash of oregano, salt, pepper and grated Parmesan cheese. Top with anchovy strips and sliced olives if desired.
4   Brown on preheated open grill, untoasted side down, for 3 minutes or until cheese melts. Serve hot.

CLAM APPETIZERS
8-12 servings

1 (3-ounce) package cream cheese
½ cup minced clams
½ teaspoon minced onion

⅛ teaspoon Worcestershire sauce
1 egg white
8 slices white bread

Preheat grill to 3 or M. Combine and mix well: cheese, clams, onion and sauce. Beat egg white until stiff and fold into mixture. If desired, remove crust from bread and cut into triangles or strips. Spread clam mixture on bread. Cook on preheated open grill for 2 minutes or until brown and puffed. Serve hot.

easy to prepare and delightful eating

GRILLED SHRIMP LOUISIANA
4 servings

1 pound uncooked shrimp, shelled
1 teaspoon Worcestershire sauce
2 tablespoons lemon juice

½ teaspoon dry mustard
¼ cup fine dry crumbs
3 tablespoons butter or margarine

1 ADVANCE PREPARATION: Remove dark veins from shrimp and rinse in cold water. Drain well. Combine sauce, lemon juice and mustard. Sprinkle over shrimp, allow to season 30 minutes in a bowl.

2 Turn dial to 3 or M and preheat grill.

3 Toss shrimp with a fork so seasoning reaches all shrimp. Dip shrimp first in crumbs and then in butter.

4 Brown shrimp on preheated open grill for 3 minutes; turn to grill other side. Serve hot on toast.

enchiladas may be prepared in advance and used as a party snack

ENCHILADAS—TEXAS VERSION
12 enchiladas

1 pound ground beef	⅛ teaspoon pepper
2 tablespoons fat	12 fresh or canned tortillas
½ cup chopped onions	
2¼ cups (No. 2 can) tomatoes	or
1 teaspoon salt	12 5-inch cornmeal griddlecakes
1 teaspoon chili powder	(page 85)
½ clove garlic	1 cup grated cheese

1 ADVANCE PREPARATION: Brown meat in fat, remove and reserve. Add onions to fat, sauté until tender, then add tomatoes, salt, chili, garlic and pepper. Simmer for 30 minutes.

2 Use tortillas or prepare cornmeal griddlecakes as directed in recipe.

3 Place tortillas or griddlecakes on plate. Spoon ¼ cup meat sauce in center. Turn ends under and roll carefully. Place in well-greased baking dish. Cover with remaining meat sauce, top with cheese. Bake 10 mintues in a hot (400° F.) oven. Serve immediately.

thrifty party food at bargain prices

LOBSTER PANCAKE ROLL-UPS
4 servings

LOBSTER FILLING:	PANCAKES:
1 cup cooked lobster meat	12 5-inch "Mighty Good"
¼ cup salad dressing	pancakes (page 80)
1 tablespoon minced pepper	
1 tablespoon minced pimiento	
1 tablespoon lemon juice	*Topping:*
¼ teaspoon A-1 sauce	1½ cups shredded cheese
⅛ teaspoon salt	½ cup milk

1 ADVANCE PREPARATION: *Lobster Filling.* Combine lobster, salad dressing, minced pepper, pimiento, lemon juice, A-1 sauce and salt. Refrigerate.

2 *Cheese Topping.* Place cheese and milk in top of a double boiler. Stir over hot water until cheese melts. This sauce will be very smooth.

3 *Pancakes.* Prepare pancakes as directed in recipe ladling each pancake with ⅓ cup measure.

4 *Lobster Roll-Ups.* In center of each pancake place 1 tablespoon filling, fold over and roll carefully. Place, seam down, in a shallow baking dish. Pour cheese topping over filled pancakes. Place under boiler for about 5 minutes until cheese melts, or serve cheese topping as an accompaniment.

this will establish your reputation as an excellent cook

HUNGARIAN LAYER PANCAKE WITH HAM
8 generous servings

1 cup commercial sour cream	PANCAKES:
1 pound cooked ham, chopped	6 8-inch "Mighty Good" pan-
2 egg yolks	cakes (page 80)
4 tablespoons butter for top	

1 ADVANCE PREPARATION: Combine sour cream, chopped ham and egg yolks. Refrigerate until ready to use.

2 Prepare pancakes as directed in recipe ladling each pancake with ¾ cup measure. Keep warm in a 300° F. oven as made.

3 Place a jumbo pancake on a buttered baking plate and spread with about 3 tablespoons ham filling. Top with another pancake, spread with ham filling and continue to stack. Dot top pancake with butter and bake layered pancakes in oven until filling is firm (about 20 minutes).

4 Cut in pie-shaped wedges and serve very hot.

suggestion for a Sunday night meal

ASSORTED PANCAKE ROLL-UPS

18 pancakes

ORANGE SAUCE:
1 8-ounce jar orange marmalade
2 tablespoons orange juice
¼ cup corn syrup

FILLING:
6 cooked sausage links
6 slices boiled ham
½ pound Philadelphia cream
cheese

PANCAKES:
1⅞ cups sifted all-purpose flour
3 tablespoons sugar
¾ teaspoon baking soda
1½ teaspoon salt
4 eggs
½ cup cold water
¾ cup cream
2 tablespoons melted fat

1   ADVANCED PREPARATION: *Orange Sauce.* Combine marmalade, orange juice and corn syrup in a sauce pan. Bring to a boil.

2   Turn dial to 3 or M to preheat griddle.

3   Sift together flour, sugar, baking soda and salt.

4   Beat eggs until light, add water. Carefully stir in sifted dry ingredients, blend with as few strokes as possible. Add cream and fat.

5   Test griddle. Using a ¼ cup measure, pour each pancake with a single, quick motion. Bake 2 minutes or until pancake is bubbly and golden brown. Turn with a spatula and bake 1 minute more. Remove "cakes" to hot platter as ready.

6   Fill center of each of 6 pancakes with a sausage link, a slice of ham and 2 tablespoons cream cheese. Roll carefully.

7   Serve a roll-up of sausage, ham and cheese for each portion. Pass orange sauce, reheated at the last minute.

PANCAKE ROLL-UPS may be prepared in advance and refrigerated. Reheat on a buttered grill. Serve with warm Orange Sauce. This is especially recommended for a Sunday night supper.

blintzes with variations are gourmet foods

CONTINENTAL CHEESE BLINTZES
12 blintzes

CHEESE FILLING:
1½ cups farmer cheese or drained
   cottage cheese
1 egg yolk
1 tablespoon sugar
1 teaspoon grated lemon rind

BATTER:
2 eggs
½ cup milk
¼ teaspoon salt
½ cup sifted all-purpose flour
1 cup sour cream
Sprinkle of cinnamon and sugar,
   optional

1 ADVANCE PREPARATION: Combine cheese, egg yolk, sugar and lemon rind. Beat until smooth. Refrigerate until used.

2 PREPARE BATTER: Beat eggs until well-blended. Add milk and salt and beat again. Continue adding flour beating until smooth.

3 Bake pancakes on preheated griddle (3 or M). Use a 2-tablespoon measure for each pancake. Bake on only one side.

4 ASSEMBLE CHEESE BLINTZES: Place 1 tablespoon filling on baked side of each pancake, fold edges and roll. Refrigerate for later use or fry immediately on buttered preheated open grill until brown. Serve hot.

5 Spread each blintz with 1 tablespoon sour cream. If desired, sprinkle with sugar and cinnamon.

ANGELLO BLINTZES: Spread pancakes with jelly instead of cheese. Roll and serve with apple sauce.

CHERRY BLINTZES: Spread cooked pancakes with cherry jam or sauce. Roll, serve with sour cream.

ITALIAN BLINTZES: Spread cooked pancakes with toasted slivered almonds. Roll; serve with jelly.

STRAWBERRY BLINTZES: Spread cooked pancakes with strawberry jam or sauce. Roll; serve with sour cream.

3 *eggs for quick and easy meals*

Ancient peoples in many lands—Egyptians, Persians, Greeks, Romans and others—regarded the egg as a symbol of good fortune. So, the modern imaginative homemaker has reason to expect good luck with eggs because they combine so well with other foods and afford a range suitable for all meals. Eggs challenge the skill of the finest French chef, yet are simple enough for any cub scout candidate for a cooking merit badge. Low to moderate temperature and a shortened cooking time spell the know-how for success.

Give eggs a break since they provide good eating and good nutrition. Use them for breakfasts to start the day right, for luncheons to keep the day going right, for adequate suppers, for formal or informal meals and snacks.

SCRAMBLED EGGS

To be perfect, scrambled eggs must be moist, tender and golden. To prepare, beat eggs with a fork only to blend, so there are streaks of yellow and a marbling of gold and white. Add milk, cream, sour cream or water for liquid. Place on buttered grill, allow the eggs to set at bottom, stir occasionally but not constantly.

Combine eggs with any number of foods such as cooked meat or poultry strips, chives, vegetables, chopped parsley, fresh or dried fine herbs, and bright bits of pimiento, green peppers and other left-over oddments. Garnish with wedges or slices of tomato, parsley, watercress, mushrooms or strips of bacon and be sure to serve hot on heated plates.

FRIED EGGS

According to experts, Americans really sauté eggs in a small amount of fat and the French fry eggs in deep fat. On the grill, eggs can be sautéed in a small amount of fat, using butter or margarine or the fat remaining from broiling bacon or ham slices.

Fried eggs should be golden brown at the edges with a crisp little crust. If preferred "sunny side up," do not turn the eggs over. If not, turn with a wide spatula or pancake turner. Break the egg in a small saucer or cup and gently slide it onto the preheated buttered grill. Serve hot on heated platter or plates.

OMELETS

The grill can be used for individual plain and fluffy omelets. The typical French omelet is prepared in a heavy pan with rounded sides not readily found in American homes, so French omelets cannot be prepared in the traditional manner. Omelets are pre-pared like scrambled eggs, just blended until yolks and whites are mixed. The egg mixture is placed on the preheated buttered grill. Instead of scrambling, it is folded after the egg becomes set, and then it is rolled. Serve hot on heated platter.

you will enjoy eggs with an Italian flavor

EGGS À LA CACCIATORA

2 servings

8 chicken livers, cut in half	4 eggs
8 mushroom caps	Butter or margarine (for grill)
3 tablespoons melted butter or margarine	Salt and pepper to taste

1 Turn dial to 3 or M and preheat grill.
2 Remove stems from mushrooms. Dip livers and mushroom caps in melted butter. Brush preheated grill with butter or margarine. Sauté livers and mushrooms until lightly browned, about 6 minutes. Reserve.
3 Beat eggs slightly, add salt and pepper. Brush grill with butter or margarine. Scramble eggs on open grill until thickened, about 3 minutes.
4 Serve eggs on heated plates; garnish with sautéed livers and mushrooms.

just right when the clock says hurry, hurry and the family is hungry

COTTAGE EGGS

4 servings

¼ pound chipped dried beef, shredded	6 eggs
2 tablespoons butter or margarine	½ cup cottage cheese
¼ cup sliced scallions	Butter or margarine

1 ADVANCE PREPARATION: Melt butter on preheated open grill. Brown beef and scallions. Reserve.
2 Turn dial to 3 or M and preheat grill.
3 Beat eggs, add cottage cheese and mix well.
4 Place dried beef and scallions on open grill. Pour beaten eggs over mixture. Stir slowly until eggs are thick for about 4 minutes. Serve hot.

attractive dish for luncheon or supper

SCRAMBLED EGGS WITH VEGETABLES

2 servings

4 eggs
¼ cup milk
½ teaspoon salt
⅛ teaspoon pepper
½ cup diced cooked carrots

1 cup hot peas, drained and
buttered
Butter or margarine
⅔ cup cooked mushrooms

1 Turn dial to 3 or M and preheat grill.
2 Prepare eggs by beating slightly, add milk, salt, pepper and diced carrots.
3 Brush grill with butter. Pour egg mixture onto open grill. When eggs begin to set, in about 4 minutes, add ½ cup peas. Do not overcook.
4 Serve scrambled eggs with remaining ½ cup peas and mushrooms.

its popularity extends East, North and South

WESTERN SCRAMBLE

4 servings

4 eggs, slightly beaten
1 cup diced cooked ham
2 tablespoons minced onion

¼ green pepper, chopped
Butter or margarine

1 Turn dial to 3 or M and preheat grill.
2 Combine eggs, ham, onion and pepper.
3 Brush grill with butter or margarine. Pour onto preheated buttered grill, stir with fork until eggs are thickened and cooked, about 3 minutes. Serve hot.

quick, easy and good—a standby for busy days

EGG CHEESEBURGERS
4 servings

2 tablespoons butter or margarine	8 thick slices American cheese,
2 tablespoons chopped green	cut to fit buns
pepper	4 eggs, lightly beaten
2 tablespoons chopped onion	½ teaspoon salt
4 buns	Butter or margarine

1 Turn dial to 3 or M and preheat grill.
2 Melt butter or margarine on preheated grill. Add green pepper and onion and cook until soft but do not brown.
3 Cut buns in half, top with slice of cheese.
4 Add beaten eggs to sautéed green pepper and onion. When eggs are scrambled, place on cheese-covered bun. Serve immediately.

prepare in advance, refrigerate until ready to use and avoid last minute rushes

EGG MUSHROOM CUTLETS
4 servings

2 cups chopped hard-cooked eggs	Salt and pepper
¾ cup medium white sauce	Cracker crumbs
¼ teaspoon grated onion	1 egg, beaten slightly
1¼ cups sliced sautéed	Butter or margarine
mushrooms	

1 ADVANCED PREPARATION: Combine eggs, white sauce, onion, mushrooms, salt and pepper. Refrigerate for 1 hour or until well chilled, to make cutlets more attractive.
2 Turn dial to 3 or M and preheat grill.

3 Shape chilled mixture into 8 cutlets. Roll in cracker crumbs. Dip in beaten egg and again in cracker crumbs.

4 Brush grill with butter or margarine. Place cutlets on preheated grill for 6 minutes or until browned. Turn to brown other side. Serve hot. Tomato sauce is an excellent accompaniment.

Chinese food, really worth the time and trouble

EGG FOO YONG
6 servings

6 eggs, well beaten

1 cup cooked, chopped shrimp, pork, chicken, turkey, lobster or crabmeat

½ cup sliced, canned mushrooms

¼ cup sliced, canned water chestnuts

½ cup bean sprouts, drained

¼ cup chopped onion

½ green pepper, chopped

1 stalk celery, chopped

1 teaspoon salt

¼ teaspoon pepper

Butter or margarine

1 Turn dial to 3 or M and preheat grill.

2 Combine eggs, chopped meat, mushrooms, chestnuts, bean sprouts, onion, pepper, celery, sauce, salt and pepper.

3 Brush grill with butter. Ladle ¼ cup of mixture onto preheated grill. Bake until golden brown on one side, about 4 minutes. With a wide spatula, gently turn and brown other side.

4 Arrange on top of cooked rice on a hot serving platter. Serve with soy sauce.

CHOW MEIN NOODLES may be obtained canned in almost any grocery store and add an interesting note to the meal instead of rice. Precooked rice cuts the cooking time and insures the perfect grains expected in an accompaniment to a Chinese dish.

add mushrooms, bacon bits, strips of chicken or ham for variety

INDIVIDUAL OMELETS

2 servings

4 eggs, separated   Dash of pepper
2 tablespoons milk   3 tablespoons butter or margarine
½ teaspoon salt

1 Turn dial to 3 or M and preheat grill.
2 Prepare omelets by beating egg whites until stiff. Reserve. Beat
   egg yolks until light, add milk, salt and pepper. Fold in egg
   whites.
3 Brush grill with butter or margarine. For individual servings,
   which are easier to handle, pour one half of the mixture on preheated grill. Then place the other serving on grill. When eggs
   are set and surface browned, turn to brown other side. Serve
   hot.

4 meats and other main dishes

Pleasing family and friends is no problem for the homemaker who serves grilled or sautéed meat. She can plan a meal for every day, for company or for any occasion—quick, easy and budget-wise meals which are fit for the king of your household.

The grill is ideal not only for cooking but also for reheating meats such as sliced tongue, roasts and servings of poultry. Small containers shaped like individual flat boats can be made of metal foil and used for reheating stews, baked beans and many other foods. Frozen French fried potatoes or other vegetables may be warmed alongside grilled hamburgers or minute steaks to make easy to cleanup meals. Kabobs on skewers are easy to grill. Originally kabobs were prepared over an open fire but the modern homemaker just opens the grill and grills indoors, for all-year enjoyment.

Pan-broiling time for meats can be estimated only and will vary with individual tastes and thickness of meat. This chart is an approximate guide.

Total cooking time in minutes

CUT	THICKNESS	RARE	MEDIUM	WELL-DONE
Steaks				
Rib, sirloin,	1″	15–20	20–25	25–30
club, T-bone,	1½″	20–25	25–30	35–40
tenderloin and	2″	25–30	30–35	35–45
porterhouse				
Lamb chops				
Rib, loin and	1″	—	10–15	15–20
shoulder	1½″	—	15–20	20–25
	2″	—	20–25	25–30
Cured Ham				
Cooked	¾–1″	—	—	10–15
Uncooked	¾–1″	—	—	20–25

Allow 6 to 8 ounces of steak, 1 large or 2 small chops or ¼ pound ham per serving portion. Arrange meat attractively on a hot serving platter and garnish with parsley, lemon, a broiled fruit, a broiled vegetable or pass a sauce.

grilled pineapple or apple rings as accompaniments

GRILLED BACON

To grill bacon, put slices on a cold grill. Turn dial to 3 or M and broil in closed grill 3 to 4 minutes to prevent curling, or until crisp. Drain on a paper towel before serving. Grill Canadian bacon in the same manner. Be sure to adjust the drip cup to accommodate the grease.

GRILLED SAUSAGE

To grill sausage, put sausage patties or links on a cold grill. Turn dial to 3 or M. Broil links on an open grill and patties in a closed grill until well-done. Turn links often. The ready-to-brown partially cooked sausage links are excellent and require less cooking time. It is imperative that sausage be cooked well-done. Be sure to adjust the drip cup to accommodate the grease.

MINUTE STEAKS

To grill fresh or frozen minute steaks, turn dial to 3 or M to preheat grill. Broil steaks on buttered grill 1 to 2 minutes or until done as desired. Frozen steaks need no defrosting.

VEAL CUTLET CHIPS
4 servings

4 veal cutlets ¼ inch thick	cheese, grated
1 egg, slightly beaten	Salt and pepper to taste
2 tablespoons milk or water	Garlic salt, optional
1 cup (¼ pound) Parmesan	Melted fat

1 Turn dial to 3 or M and preheat grill.
2 Prepare veal cutlets by pounding, until thin and flat. Season with garlic salt, salt and pepper to taste. Combine egg and milk or water. Dip cutlets in egg-milk mixture, then in grated cheese.
3 Brush grill with melted fat. Grill veal 8 minutes or until delicately browned. Turn and grill other side.
4 Serve veal cutlet chips on spaghetti. Top with mushroom-tomato sauce. Serve hot.

prepare in advance and grill at the table

BEEF ROLLS EN BROCHETTE
4 servings

1 pound chopped beef	½ teaspoon minced parsley
½ teaspoon salt	2 tablespoons sour cream
¼ teaspoon paprika	4 slices bacon
Pepper to taste	

1 ADVANCE PREPARATION: To the chopped beef add salt, paprika, pepper, parsley and sour cream. Mix well. Shape into 4 small meat loaves. Wrap the bacon slice around the flattened beef roll. Refrigerate until ready to use.
2 Turn dial to 3 or M and preheat grill.
3 Run metal skewers through beef rolls to hold the bacon strip in place. Cook on preheated open grill for 5 minutes or until done on one side. Turn, and grill the other side as desired. Serve hot with a meat sauce.

this should win you the coveted blue ribbon

STEAK DIANE
4 servings

4 thin strips sirloin steak (4 inches by 8 inches)	¼ cup chopped parsley
	1 lemon quartered
¼ cup salad oil	Worcestershire sauce
1 clove garlic, minced	Freshly ground pepper

1 Brush steak strips with salad oil to which garlic has been added. Allow steak to stand a few minutes and brush again with salad oil.
2 Turn dial to 3 or M and preheat grill.
3 Brown steaks on preheated open grill (additional melted fat

is unnecessary), for 3 minutes or until done as you like it. Turn and grill other side. Sprinkle with chopped parsley.

4 Serve very hot with lemon juice, Worcestershire sauce and fresh pepper.

prepare beefburgers in advance and refrigerate until grilling time

BEEFBURGERS
4 servings

1 pound ground beef	1 tablespoon catsup
1 small onion, minced	1 teaspoon garlic salt
1 egg, slightly beaten	¼ teaspoon Worcestershire sauce
1 teaspoon salt	4 slices bacon
¼ teaspoon pepper	Melted butter or margarine
1 teaspoon prepared mustard	4 buns

1 Turn dial to 3 or M and preheat grill.
2 Combine meat, onion, egg, salt, pepper, mustard, catsup, garlic and Worcestershire sauce. Mix thoroughly. Shape into 4 patties about ¾ inch thick. Wrap a strip of bacon around each. Fasten with a toothpick.
3 Brush grill with melted butter. Broil beefburgers on preheated greased open grill for 10 minutes or until browned as desired. Turn and grill 10 minutes longer.
4 Cut buns in half. Place cut-side down on grill to heat for last 5 minutes. Serve immediately.

BARBECUED BEEFBURGERS: Prepare beefburgers and allow to marinate in barbecue sauce for 10 minutes. Drain. Broil as directed, brush with barbecue sauce when beefburgers are ready to serve.

CHEESEBURGERS: Prepare beefburgers as directed. When almost ready to serve, place a slice of American cheese on each patty. Serve when cheese begins to melt.

left-overs can be used with this combination to advantage

MEAT AND POTATO DUETS
6 servings

2 cups cooked ground meat
1 cup mashed potatoes
1 tablespoon catsup
1 tablespoon minced onion

1 teaspoon prepared mustard
½ teaspoon salt
Melted fat

1   Turn dial to 3 or M and preheat grill.
2   Combine meat, potatoes, catsup, onion, mustard and salt. When well mixed, shape into patties ¾ inch thick. Allow to stand a few minutes.
3   Brush grill with melted fat. Broil on preheated grill for 5 minutes or until well browned. Turn to grill other side.
4   Place on a heated platter or plates.

substitute canned corned beef hash for beef and potatoes

CORNED BEEF HASH CAKES
6-8 cakes

2 cups cooked chopped corned
   beef
1 cup mashed potatoes
2 tablespoons minced onion
1 teaspoon prepared mustard

¼ teaspoon Worcestershire sauce
Salt and pepper to taste
⅓ cup milk
Melted fat

1   Turn dial to 3 or M and preheat grill.
2   Combine corned beef, potatoes, onion, mustard, sauce, salt, pepper and milk. When well blended, shape into cakes about ¾ inch thick.
3   Brush grill with melted fat. Brown cakes on preheated open grill 5 minutes, turn and brown other side.

4 Place on heated serving platter, garnish with parsley if desired.

WITH POACHED EGG. Make a depression on top of cake for poached egg and place it in the hollow when ready to serve.

grills are easy and enjoyable

ENGLISH MIXED GRILL
2 servings

2 lamb chops	4 mushroom caps
4 sausages	Melted butter or margarine
4 slices bacon	

1 Turn dial to 3 or M and preheat grill.
2 Prepare lamb chops by cutting fat around edges and removing bones.
3 Broil lamb chops and sausages on preheated grill for about 10 minutes. Turn to brown other side. Add bacon slices to broil and brown. Brush mushroom caps with butter and place on heated grill. Turn bacon and sausage to brown.
4 Place lamb chops on a heated platter. Drain bacon slices on a paper towel before serving. Arrange sausage, bacon and mushroom caps on a heated platter with lamb chops. Serve hot.

MINUTE STEAK MIXED GRILL: Substitute minute steaks and apricot halves for lamb chops and sausages.

CALVES LIVER MIXED GRILL: Substitute calves liver and apple rings for lamb chops and sausages. Serve with mushroom sauce.

planned for hearty and discriminating appetites

LAMB KIDNEY AND SAUSAGE GRILL
4 servings

8 lamb kidneys	Salt and pepper
Melted butter or margarine	8 apricot halves
8 sausage links	Parsley
4 tomatoes, cut in slices	

1 Turn dial to 3 or M and preheat grill.
2 Split kidneys, remove fat and veins. Wash. Dip in butter.
3 Brush preheated grill with butter. Brown kidneys and sausage links on preheated open grill for 6 minutes. When kidneys and sausage are done on one side, turn and brown other side. Brush tomatoes with butter, season with salt and pepper. Place on grill alongside lamb for last 3 minutes. Brush apricots with butter, warm on grill. Serve mixed grill on heated plates. Garnish with parsley.

SWEETBREAD AND MUSHROOM GRILL. Substitute cooked, cleaned sweetbreads and mushrooms for lamb kidneys and sausage links. Garnish with lemon.

weight-watchers grill: lamb chops and tomato slices

MINTED LAMB CHOPS
2 or 4 servings

4 lamb chops, each ¾ inch thick   ¼ cup mint jelly
Salt and pepper

1 Turn dial to 3 or M and preheat grill.
2 Prepare lamb chops by removing the thin fell covering the fat. Snip or slash the fat in several places to prevent curling.

3 Grill on preheated grill about 8 minutes until browned. Turn chops to brown the other side. Close grill and broil 8 minutes, if preferred.

4 Place on heated serving platter or plates. Season with salt and pepper. Spread each chop with 1 teaspoon mint jelly. If chops are small, serve two for each person.

a Mediterranean favorite for your table

GREEK KABOBS WITH RICE
6 servings

1½ pounds lean lamb
1 cup French dressing
12 stuffed olives
6 slices bacon, cut in half
12 mushroom caps

3 tomatoes, quartered
3 onions, quartered
1 green pepper, cut in 12 pieces
Melted fat

1 ADVANCE PREPARATION: Cut lamb into 1½ inch cubes and marinate in French dressing for 1 hour.

2 Turn dial to 3 or M and preheat grill.

3 Prepare kabobs by wrapping olives in bacon slices, alternating meat, mushrooms, tomato, onion, green pepper and bacon-wrapped olives on 6 metal skewers. Brush with remaining French dressing.

4 Brush grill with melted fat. Broil on preheated open grill for 8 minutes or until meat is browned, turn to brown all sides.

5 Slide meat and vegetables from skewers onto heated platter. Serve with Turkish pilaf. (Cook 1½ cups washed raw rice in 3½ cups salted water and ½ cup butter.)

PILAF may be prepared with sautéed onion and sprinkled with pine-nuts when served. If the kabobs are served with fluffy rice, it is a treat. The processed and the precooked rices, available in any grocery store, guarantee perfect rice.

CAUCASIAN KABOB. Substitute cubes of eggplant or chunks of pineapple for green pepper and tomato.

popular with cook and family

SWEETBREADS EN BROCHETTE
4 servings

1 pound cooked sweetbreads	8 slices green pepper
Salt and pepper to taste	Melted butter or margarine
4 slices bacon	4 slices buttered toast
12 mushrooms, optional	

1 ADVANCE PREPARATION: Cut sweetbreads into 1 inch cubes. Season with salt and pepper. Cut bacon into 1 inch slices. Remove stems from mushrooms.

2 Turn dial to 3 or M and preheat grill.

3 Alternate sweetbread cubes, bacon slices, mushrooms and green peppers on metal skewers. Dip in melted butter.

4 Brush preheated grill with melted butter. Lightly brown sweetbreads en brochette on open grill for about 5 minutes. Turn, and brown on other side for 5 minutes. Serve very hot on slices of buttered toast.

good-together flavors

HAM AND PINEAPPLE HAWAIIAN
4 servings

½ inch thick slice of center cut ham	2 tablespoons butter or margarine
4 bananas, cut in half lengthwise	4 toasted English muffins or 4 waffles
4 slices drained pineapple	Maple syrup

1 Turn dial to 3 or M and preheat grill.

2 Broil ham on open grill until browned on both sides, turning once. Transfer to warm platter. Sauté banana slices and pineapple rings.

3 Cut grilled ham into 4 servings. Place a serving on each toasted muffin or waffle, top with pineapple ring. Serve grilled banana half alongside ham.

a special entrée for a red letter occasion

CHICKEN AND ALMONDS PATRICIA

1 green pepper, cut into thin strips
1 small onion, cut into thin slices
2½ cups cooked chicken, cut into long strips

5 mushrooms, sliced
1 cup almonds, shredded
5 tablespoons butter or margarine
1½ cups hot cooked rice

1 Turn dial to 3 or M and preheat grill.
2 Spread butter on preheated grill and sauté green pepper and onion rings slightly. Add chicken; cook, turning, until lightly browned. If mushrooms are fresh add with chicken; if canned add with almonds. Add almonds and heat thoroughly. If necessary, add more butter to keep slightly moist. Serve immediately as a topping for hot buttered rice.

an unusual and easily prepared treat

GRILLED CHICKEN LIVERS AND MUSHROOMS
4 servings

1 pound chicken livers, fresh or frozen
4 fresh mushrooms or 12 canned mushroom caps

3 tablespoons melted butter or margarine
Salt and pepper to taste
4 slices buttered toast

1 ADVANCE PREPARATION: Prepare the chicken livers by separating if they are large. Wipe livers with a damp cloth. Brush with melted butter.
2 Turn the dial to 3 or M and preheat grill.
3 Brush the preheated grill with melted butter. Place the chicken livers on the grill for 5 minutes, turn when brown. Slice the mushrooms and add to the grill. Turn the mushrooms so that both sides are sautéed.
4 Serve the grilled chicken livers and sautéed mushrooms on the buttered toast.

turkey steaks streamlined for your grill

STUFFED TURKEY STEAKS STELLA
4 servings

2 tablespoons butter or margarine	4 4-ounce turkey steaks, defrosted
½ cup chopped celery	¼ cup flour
1 tablespoon chopped onion	1 teaspoon salt
½ cup whole kernel corn	1 teaspoon paprika
½ cup fine dry crumbs	¼ cup butter or margarine,
½ teaspoon salt	melted
1 egg	

1 Turn dial to 3 or M and preheat grill.
2 Spread butter on preheated grill and sauté celery and onion. When slightly browned, remove and use in stuffing.
3 In mixing bowl combine sautéed celery, onion, corn, crumbs, salt and egg. Divide stuffing and spread on turkey steaks. Roll. Fasten with toothpicks. Roll turkey steaks in flour seasoned with salt and paprika.
4 Brush turkey steaks and grill with melted butter. Brown turkey for 10 minutes. Turn often until well-browned on all sides. Serve very hot.

often served in Brazil and Portugal

PORTUGUESE TURKEY PANCAKES
6 servings

6 slices turkey, light meat	12 5-inch "Mighty Good"
6 slices turkey, dark meat	pancakes (page 80)
1 cup medium cream sauce	

1 Cut turkey slices lengthwise. Arrange slice of dark meat and slice of light meat for each pancake. Reserve.
2 Pancakes: Prepare pancakes as directed in recipe and assemble roll-ups from warm pancakes.

3 In center of each pancake place 1 tablespoon of cream sauce and strip of light and dark turkey meat. Roll carefully. Return to grill to warm and serve immediately.

TURKEY PANCAKES WITH CHEESE. Prepare as directed and place pancakes in buttered baking dish. Sprinkle with 1½ cups grated cheese. Bake in moderate oven 350° F. for 20 minutes or until cheese melts. Serve immediately.

a very successful combination

CHIPPED BEEF AND BUCKWHEAT ROLL-UPS
4 servings

2 tablespoons butter or margarine	2 tablespoons chopped parsley
¼ pound shredded chipped beef	4-inch Buckwheat pancakes
2 tablespoons all-purpose flour	(recipe page 82)
1 cup milk	

1 ADVANCE PREPARATION: *Chipped Beef Sauce.* Melt butter in a saucepan, add shredded beef and sauté until lightly browned. Blend in flour and milk. Cook over low fire until sauce is thick and smooth. Reserve. Just before serving, add chopped parsley.
2 Prepare pancakes as directed in recipe.
3 To assemble roll-ups, fill pancakes with heated creamed chipped beef sauce. Shape pancakes into cones. Secure with toothpick.
4 Place on grill to reheat. Serve hot.

CHIPPED BEEF AND BUCKWHEAT PIE. For individual service, stack 4-inch pancakes with chipped beef sauce between each one. Or prepare large pancakes in the same manner and cut large pie into four servings.

the specialty featured in a famous New York restaurant

PANCAKES FILLED WITH CHICKEN HASH

6 *servings*

FILLING:
2 tablespoons melted butter
2 tablespoons lemon juice
2 cups left-over chicken
4 tablespoons chopped mush-
    rooms
½ teaspoon salt
4 tablespoons cream

PANCAKES:
12 8-inch "Mighty Good"
    pancakes (page 80)

TOPPING:
1 cup grated Parmesan cheese

1   To prepare hash, combine melted butter, lemon juice, coarsely chopped chicken, mushrooms and salt. Cook for a few minutes to heat and add cream. Reserve to use when assembling pancake roll-ups.

2   Pancakes: Prepare pancakes as directed in recipe.

3   In center of each pancake place ¼ cup chicken hash. Roll carefully. Place pancakes in buttered baking dish, seam side down. Sprinkle top of pancakes with cheese. Bake in moderate oven (350° F.) for 15 minutes. Serve very hot.

HAM, TURKEY OR MEAT HASH may be used with pancakes in the manner of the above recipe. The addition of sautéed mushrooms and lemon juice will improve the hash and make it better suited to use. Add cream or gravy to be certain that the hash is not dry. You will find this is a likely candidate for a family favorite.

waffles are an excellent foundation for curried chicken or meat

CHICKEN CURRY ON WAFFLES
6 servings

TOPPING:
1 cup chopped onion
½ clove of garlic
¼ cup chopped apple
2 tablespoons fat
½ teaspoon salt
½ teaspoon curry
3 tablespoons all-purpose flour
2 cups chicken stock
½ cup milk
1 cup diced cooked chicken

WAFFLES:
Favorite Waffle recipe
or Pancake Quick Mix

Curry Accompaniments:
Sieved hard-cooked egg yolks, chutney, coconut, chopped peanuts, crisp bacon strips, chopped sweet pickle. Use a small bowl for each.

1 ADVANCE PREPARATION: Cook onion, garlic and apple in butter until tender. Add salt, curry, milk, stock, and flour. Blend well. Cook until thick, stirring constantly. Add chicken and heat thoroughly.
2 Prepare waffles as directed in recipe.
3 Place heated curry mixture on crisp hot waffles. Serve immediately.
4 Serve Chicken Curry with several of the accompaniments in small bowls as garnish.

5 *grilled fish and shellfish*

Fish is one of the oldest foods known to man and according to surveys, second only to steaks in popularity at cafés and restaurants. Grilling is an ideal method for preparing this staple food. Fish cooks easier and quicker than meat as there are no muscles that require tenderizing by long, slow cooking. Overcooking fish for too long and at too high a temperature is the mistake the less experienced cook usually makes. If you observe fish, it tells you when done, moist and flavorful. When the semi-transparent color changes to golden brown or pearly white, and the flesh can be flaked with a fork, it is ready to serve. Cooking fish on a table grill makes observation easier.

Menus featuring fish must include other foods for accompaniment. Salads of greens, mixed vegetables, cole slaw with sharp, tart dressings are essential. Garnishes, such as crisp celery, cucumbers, green peppers, lemon and lime wedges (for easier juicing), parsley, pimiento, radishes, tomatoes, watercress, various pickles and relishes are welcome.

prepared on metal skewers like kabobs

SHRIMP EN BROCHETTE

4 servings

20 large shrimp	¼ cup French dressing
12 slices bacon, cut in half	

1 ADVANCE PREPARATION: Cook shrimp in boiling salted water until shells turn pink (about 10 minutes). Drain. Peel off shells and remove dark veins. Place in bowl with French dressing to season for 30 minutes. Drain well.
2 Turn dial to 3 or M and preheat grill.
3 On 4 metal skewers, alternate 6 folded slices of bacon and 5 shrimp. Begin and finish with bacon.
4 Cook on preheated grill for about 3 minutes or until bacon is done. Turn to grill other side. Serve hot.

add mushrooms on the skewers for an extra

OYSTER KABOBS

4 servings

10 slices bacon, cut in half	Melted butter or margarine
16 medium oysters	Salt and pepper to taste
3 firm tomatoes, cut in quarters	

1 Turn dial to 3 or M and preheat grill.
2 On each of the 4 skewers, string ingredients in this order: folded bacon slice, oyster, tomato quarter. Each skewer has in total 5 half slices bacon, 4 oysters, 4 tomato quarters. Brush ingredients with melted butter or margarine. Season with salt and pepper.
3 Brush grill with melted fat. Place skewers on preheated open grill and broil 3 minutes or until bacon is crisp. Turn and grill other side until bacon is crisp and oyster edges curl.

outdoor picnic favorites brought to the dining table

ANGELS ON HORSEBACK
6 *servings*

24 large oysters	⅛ teaspoon pepper
12 slices bacon, cut in half	⅛ teaspoon paprika
½ teaspoon salt	2 tablespoons chopped parsley

1 Turn dial to 3 or M and preheat grill.
2 Place a drained oyster in the center of each half slice of bacon. Sprinkle with seasoning and chopped parsley. Roll bacon around oyster and fasten with a toothpick.
3 Pan-broil bacon-wrapped oysters on preheated open grill 4 minutes or until bacon is well done. Turn and brown other side. Remove toothpicks. Serve hot.

a Dixie favorite

SOUTHERN CRABBURGERS
6 *servings*

2 cups cooked flaked crabmeat	½ teaspoon dry mustard
1 cup thick white sauce	1 teaspoon salt
½ cup fine bread crumbs	¼ teaspoon pepper
2 teaspoons minced onion	Melted fat

1 ADVANCE PREPARATION: Combine crabmeat, sauce, bread crumbs, onion, mustard, salt and pepper. Refrigerate 1 hour so crabburgers will be well seasoned and will hold shape when cooked.
2 Turn dial to 3 or M and preheat grill.
3 Brush preheated grill with melted fat. Place 4 tablespoons (¼ cup measure) crabburger mixture on preheated greased grill. Bake on open grill for 5 minutes on each side or until golden brown. Serve hot.

a prize catch for an easy meal

GRILLED FISH WITH HERBS
4 servings

4 fish steaks, each ¾-inch thick
1 tablespoon grated onion
Juice of 1 lemon
2 tablespoons melted butter or margarine

½ teaspoon salt
¼ teaspoon pepper
½ teaspoon marjoram
2 tablespoons minced parsley
2 tablespoons melted fat

1   Turn dial to 3 or M and preheat grill.
2   Combine: onion, lemon, butter or margarine, salt, pepper and herbs. Spread ½ of mixture on fish steaks. Turn steaks and spread with remaining mixture.
3   Brush grill with melted fat. Sauté fish steaks on preheated open grill for 8 minutes or until they are golden brown and can be flaked with the tip of a fork. Serve hot on heated plate.

DEVILED FISH STEAKS
4 servings

1½ pounds cod, halibut, salmon or swordfish steak slices, ¾ inch thick
2 tablespoons prepared mustard
1 tablespoon salad oil

2 tablespoons chili sauce
2 tablespoons horseradish
1 teaspoon salt
Melted fat

1   ADVANCE PREPARATION: Allow frozen fish steaks to thaw for at least 20 minutes and add 2 or 3 minutes to cooking time.
2   Turn dial to 3 or M and preheat grill.
3   Combine: mustard, oil, chili sauce, horseradish and salt. Spread half of mixture on one side of fish steaks.
4   Brush grill with melted fat. Place seasoned side of steaks on grill. Cook on open grill for 6 minutes or until browned. Turn, spread with remaining seasoning and grill until browned.

unusual, easily prepared and ever so delicious

LOBSTER MIGNON
6 servings

3 frozen (10 oz. each) lobster tails	2 tablespoons melted butter or margarine
6 large stuffed olives	Salt, pepper, paprika to taste
6 slices bacon	1 teaspoon chopped chives

1 ADVANCE PREPARATION: Allow lobster to thaw about 45 minutes. Cut undershell membranes with kitchen scissors. Split tails in half.

2 Turn dial to 3 or M and preheat grill.

3 On each halved lobster tail, place an olive and wrap with a slice of bacon. Fasten with a skewer or toothpick. Brush with butter.

4 Cook lobster on preheated open grill for 3 minutes or until flesh is opaque, turn and grill other side. Season to taste with salt, pepper and paprika. Sprinkle with chopped chives. Serve hot.

cutlets may be prepared earlier and used when needed

SALMON CUTLETS
6 servings

1 cup thick white sauce	2 tablespoons lemon juice
1 egg yolk	3 tablespoons minced parsley
½ teaspoon salt	1 egg plus 1 tablespoon water
⅛ teaspoon pepper	1 cup fine crumbs
2 cups cooked salmon	3 tablespoons melted fat

1 Combine white sauce, egg yolk, salt, pepper, salmon, lemon juice and parsley. Refrigerate 1 hour so cutlets will hold shape during cooking.

2 Turn dial to 3 or M and preheat closed grill.

3 Shape chilled salmon mixture into flat cutlets, allowing about ½ cup for each one. Slightly beat egg and add water. Dip cutlets in egg-water mixture. Roll in fine crumbs.

4 Brush grill with melted fat. Brown cutlets on preheated open grill for 5 minutes. Turn and grill other side. Serve hot.

LOBSTER CUTLET. Substitute lobster for salmon.

CRABMEAT CUTLET. Substitute crabmeat for salmon.

TUNA CUTLET. Substitute tuna for salmon.

an economical family favorite

TUNA PANCAKE PIE
4 servings

TUNA FILLING:
1 can (7 oz.) tuna, drained
1 can condensed mushroom soup
½ cup milk
½ teaspoon minced onion
1 tablespoon pimiento strips
1 teaspoon lemon juice

½ teaspoon salt
PANCAKES:
8 5-inch Rich Golden Pancakes (page 81)

FOR TOPPING:
1 cup (¼ pound) grated cheese

1 ADVANCE PREPARATION: *Tuna Filling.* Combine: tuna, soup, milk, onion, pimiento, lemon juice and salt. Stir until smooth and cook until well blended. Reserve.

2 Prepare pancakes as directed.

3 *Tuna Pancake Pie.* Place a pancake in slightly buttered baking pan. Spread ¼ of tuna filling over pancake. Add another pancake and continue layer cake style. End with a plain pancake. Sprinkle top with grated cheese. Bake in moderate oven (350° F.) for 15 minutes.

4 Cut into four pie-shaped wedges. Serve hot.

waffles are glamorized with shrimp and Creole Sauce

WAFFLES WITH CREOLE SHRIMP
4 servings

CREOLE SAUCE:
½ cup chopped onion
¼ cup chopped green pepper
2 tablespoons fat
1 cup undiluted tomato soup
2 tablespoons catsup
⅓ cup water

SHRIMP:
1½ pounds cooked, cleaned
  shrimp

WAFFLES:
8 Wonderful Waffles (page 94)

1 ADVANCE PREPARATION: Sauté onion and pepper in fat in a saucepan until tender. Add soup, catsup and water. Simmer 10 minutes over low heat. Stir occasionally. Before serving add shrimp and heat for 5 minutes.
2 Prepare waffles as directed.
3 Arrange waffles on individual plates. Spoon hot Creole-Shrimp Sauce on each one. Cover with 4 waffles and top with remaining Creole-Shrimp Sauce. Serve immediately.

CHEESE SAUCE may be used instead of Creole Sauce for a topping for the shrimp. You will find that strips of pimiento add interest in both color and flavor to this food.

an old-time New England favorite

CODFISH CAKES
4 servings

2 cups cooked codfish
1 cup cooked mashed potatoes
2 tablespoons melted butter
1 tablespoon minced onion
2 tablespoons minced green
  pepper

2 tablespoons chopped pimiento
Salt and pepper to taste
½ cup flour
Melted fat
Tomato sauce

1 Turn dial to 3 or M and preheat grill.
2 Combine: codfish, potatoes, butter, onion, green pepper, pimiento, salt and pepper. Mix well. Shape in cakes ½ inch thick, dip into flour to coat.
3 Brush preheated grill with fat. Sauté codfish cakes on open grill for 5 minutes or until brown. Turn, brown other side. Serve with tomato sauce on heated platter.

LEFT-OVER FISH may be used as above and shaped into flat cakes, dipped into flour and placed onto a preheated grill to sauté on both sides. Do select a sauce to add both color and flavor. Garnish attractively with parsley, watercress or some crisp salad green. So good that no one will suspect that you are pinching pennies at this meal.

kippers are partially precooked

KIPPERED HERRING
6 servings

2 pounds "kippers"	margarine
Juice 1 lemon	Pepper to taste
4 tablespoons melted butter or	

1 Turn dial to 3 or M and preheat grill.
2 Split kippers without breaking back skin. Brush opened surface with lemon juice and butter. Season with pepper.
3 Brush preheated grill with melted fat. Place kippers on greased open grill, skin side down, for about 4 minutes or until heated thoroughly. Serve immediately.

6 *fruits and vegetables are fun to grill*

Fruits and vegetables, grilled to accompany meats, fish and eggs, add attractive shape, color and texture to a meal. Grilled apple rings and pineapple are naturals for ham or pork in any form. Peach, pear or apricot halves add flavor and interest, especially when a tart and colorful jelly, such as mint or currant, attractively fills the cavities.

To heat cooked or canned vegetables for serving, place them in shallow metal pans or in aluminum foil containers. Heat on a preheated open grill set at 3 or M for about 10 minutes or until vegetables are ready to serve.

Canned whole kernel corn, squash, asparagus, beet slices, baked beans, sauerkraut, mixed vegetables and spinach with butter and seasonings added are quickly heated on an open grill. Dramatizing vegetables by heating them at the table may even result in a cleaner plate at Junior's setting!

a gala touch, fun to cook and excellent with meats and poultry

FLAVORFUL VEGETABLE KABOBS

6 servings

1 large eggplant, pared, cut into ½-inch cubes

12 small cooked potatoes, cut in half

3 green peppers, cut into 6ths

12 small onions

½ pound mushroom caps, stems removed

¼ cup French dressing or tomato sauce

Melted butter or margarine

1 Turn dial to 3 or M and preheat grill.

2 Alternate vegetables on 6 metal skewers. Dip in French dressing or tomato sauce.

3 Brush preheated grill with melted butter. Pan-broil kabobs on preheated open grill for 5 minutes or until vegetables are lightly browned, brushing several times with French dressing. Turn skewers as necessary. Serve very hot with meat or on top of buttered rice.

KABOB EXPERTS suggest placing all the vegetables of one kind on one skewer. In this manner each vegetable may be cooked to the desired degree of doneness. Then all may be assembled on the serving plates in the variety mentioned above. Either method of assembling vegetables is successful so choose the one that appeals to you.

an excellent accompaniment for fried chicken

DIXIE FRESH CORN CAKES
12 3-inch cakes

⅓ cup sifted all-purpose flour
½ teaspoon baking powder
¼ teaspoon salt
1 teaspoon sugar

1 egg
1 cup grated raw corn
3 tablespoons milk
3 tablespoons melted fat

1 Turn dial to 3 or M and preheat griddle.
2 Sift together: flour, baking powder, salt and sugar.
3 Beat egg until light. Add corn, milk and melted fat. Mix well.
4 Gradually add sifted dry ingredients to egg-corn-milk-fat mixture. Do not overmix. Batter should be lumpy.
5 Test griddle. Ladle each cake with a ¼ cup measure. Pour with a single, quick motion. Bake 2 minutes or until corn cake bubbles and is golden brown. Turn and bake 1 minute more.

Minced frozen whole kernel corn may be used when fresh corn is not available. It is possible that additional milk, perhaps a tablespoonful, will be needed to give pouring consistency to the batter.

everyone will say "delicious" and ask for more

FLUFFY CORN FRITTERS
4 servings

1½ cups sifted all-purpose flour
1 teaspoon salt
3 teaspoons baking powder
2 eggs, separated
¾ cup milk

½ cup melted fat
2 tablespoons sliced pimiento
1 cup cream-style corn
Butter or margarine

1 Turn dial to 5 or H and preheat grill.
2 Sift dry ingrendients: flour, salt and baking powder into mixing bowl.
3 Beat egg whites until stiff. Reserve. Beat egg yolks, add milk, melted fat, pimiento and corn. Add to sifted dry ingredients. Blend carefully. Fold in stiffly beaten egg whites.
4 Brush preheated grill with butter or margarine. Drop fritter mixture by tablespoonfuls on preheated open grill and bake for 4 minutes or until underside is well browned. Turn and brown other side. Serve very hot.

Canned whole kernel or cooked frozen corn may be used instead of the cream-style corn. This will necessitate adding one or two tablespoons of milk so the mixture will be the correct consistency for dropping by tablespoonfuls.

eggplant and cheese are an especially tasty combination

SAUTÉED EGGPLANT
4 servings

1 large eggplant, pared	2 tablespoons chopped parsley
Melted butter or margarine	¼ cup grated Parmesan cheese
Salt and pepper to taste	

1 ADVANCE PREPARATION: Cut eggplant into ½ inch slices crosswise. Cover with boiling water, allow to stand for 5 minutes. Drain and dry.
2 Turn dial to 3 or M and preheat grill.
3 Brush grill with melted butter. Sauté eggplant on preheated open or closed grill for 3 minutes or until light brown on both sides. Drain on paper towel for a moment.
4 Sprinkle with salt, pepper, parsley and cheese. Serve very hot.

serve with meats, eggs, fish and cheese

STUFFED MUSHROOMS

4 servings

12 large mushrooms	2 tablespoons melted fat
3 tablespoons butter or margarine	Salt and pepper
2 tablespoons minced onion	2 tablespoons dry crumbs

1 Turn dial to 3 or M and preheat grill.

2 Wash mushrooms. Remove stems and chop fine. Reserve mushroom caps.

3 Melt butter or margarine in saucepan, add chopped mushroom stems and minced onion. Sauté until golden brown. Add bread crumbs; stir to combine.

4 Brush mushrooms with melted butter; sprinkle with salt and pepper. Pan-broil cup side down on preheated open grill for 5 minutes or until lightly browned. Remove from grill.

5 With a spoon, fill caps with sautéed mixture. Return to open grill for about 5 minutes, this time cup side up. Serve hot.

savory and satisfying as a meat accompaniment

SAUTÉED ONION

4 servings

4 medium sized onions	Salt and pepper to taste
Melted butter or margarine	

1 Turn dial to 3 or M and preheat grill.

2 Cut onions into ¼ inch slices. If you prefer rings, separate slices. Brush with melted butter. Otherwise, use a wide pancake turner in handling so slices remain compact.

3 Brush grill with melted butter. Transfer onion slices to preheated grill. Sauté for 4 minutes or until onion begins to soften and brown. Turn, and sauté other side. Onions will be soft but not crisp. Serve hot.

61

make use of the short season of new potatoes

PARSLEYED NEW POTATOES
6 servings

12 cooked new potatoes   Salt and pepper to taste
3 tablespoons butter or margarine   3 tablespoons minced parsley

1 ADVANCE PREPARATION: Cook potatoes in their jackets. Peel
2 Turn dial to 3 or M and preheat grill.
3 Brush grill with butter or margarine. Cook potatoes on grill
   about 4 minutes or until brown on all sides. Season with salt
   and pepper; sprinkle with minced parsley. Serve hot.

an old standby—prepared in a few minutes

COUNTRY POTATOES
4 servings

6 cooked, cold potatoes or yams   Salt and pepper to taste
3 tablespoons butter or margarine

1 Turn dial to 3 or M and preheat grill.
2 Peel potatoes. Cut yams crosswise into slices ¼ inch thick.
   Brush grill with butter or margarine. Brown slices on preheated
   open grill for 2 minutes. Turn and brown other side. Sprinkle
   with salt. Serve hot.

COUNTRY POTATOES WITH ONION AND GREEN PEPPER. Sauté cold potatoes, with 2 tablespoons minced onion and 2 tablespoons minced
green pepper.

LEFT-OVER POTATOES may be shaped into flat cakes, dusted with
flour and placed upon the preheated buttered grill to brown on
both sides. To shape the cakes readily, mash the potatoes and add
a few tablespoons milk.

serve with applesauce, pot roast, or sour cream

POTATO PANCAKES
6 servings

4 medium sized potatoes
1 small onion
½ cup milk
1 teaspoon salt

1 egg, beaten
2 tablespoons all-purpose flour
Melted butter or margarine

1   ADVANCE PREPARATION: Peel and grate potatoes and onions.
2   Turn dial to 3 or M and preheat grill.
3   Combine grated potato, onion, milk and salt. Mix well. Blend in egg and flour. Mix carefully but do not overmix.
4   Brush grill generously with butter or margarine. Drop batter by tablespoonfuls on preheated griddle. Bake on open grill for 3 minutes or until brown on underside. Turn with a spatula to brown second side. Serve immediately, potato pancakes get soggy if they stand.

tender summer squash so appetizing when sautéed

SAUTÉED SQUASH CUBES
6 servings

3 tender summer squash
3 tablespoons butter or margarine

¼ teaspoon salt
Dash of pepper

1   Turn dial to 3 or M and preheat grill.
2   Prepare squash by removing seeds and cutting into 1-inch cubes. If very tender, it is unnecessary to peel squash.
3   Brush grill generously with butter or margarine. Sauté cubes on open grill about 5 minutes or until tender and lightly browned. Season with salt and pepper. Serve hot.

SAUTÉED SQUASH CUBES WITH HERBS. Prepare as directed in recipe above but sprinkle with minced fresh herbs such as chives, parsley or mint just before serving.

unusual, delicious and simple to prepare

SWEET POTATO NESTS
4 servings

2½ cups cooked, mashed sweet potatoes	½ cup crushed pineapple
Melted butter or margarine	2 tablespoons brown sugar
	Sprinkle of cinnamon

1 Turn dial to 3 or M and preheat grill.
2 Brush grill with melted butter. Divide sweet potatoes into four equal parts and shape each one as a nest with a hollow in the center. Place on preheated buttered grill. Fill centers with crushed pineapple. Sprinkle pineapple with brown sugar and cinnamon. Grill for 5 minutes or until thoroughly heated. Serve hot. Especially good with ham and roasts.

serve grilled tomatoes with eggs, fish, meat, and cheese dishes

GRILLED TOMATOES
4 servings

2 large firm tomatoes	Salt and pepper to taste
Melted butter or margarine	Sprinkle of curry powder, optional
Fine bread crumbs	

1 Turn dial to 3 or M and preheat grill.
2 Cut tomatoes into ½ inch slices. Brush with melted butter. Top with bread crumbs; sprinkle with salt and pepper; dot with butter. Place in preheated closed grill for 2 minutes or until crumbs brown slightly. Serve very hot.

grilled fruits added to meats are ideal quick meals

GRILLED APPLES

3 firm apples, unpared   Melted butter or margarine
Lemon juice

1 Turn dial to 3 or M and preheat grill.
2 Cut apple into ½ inch slices or wedges. Remove core. Dip in lemon juice to prevent discoloring, then into melted butter.
3 Brush grill with butter. Sauté apple slices on preheated open grill for 3 minutes or until delicately brown. Turn; brown other side. Serve hot with ham, pork, and roast.

GRILLED BANANAS. Select firm bananas, cut lengthwise. Wrap each half in bacon and fasten with a toothpick. Sauté for 3 minutes on open grill. Turn; brown other side. Serve hot.

GRILLED PINEAPPLE RINGS OR SPEARS. Drain pineapple rings or spears. Brush with melted butter. Place on preheated open grill and sauté, turning once. Sprinkle with brown sugar. Serve hot.

GRILLED PEARS, PEACHES AND APRICOTS. Drain fruit. Brush with melted butter and roll in chopped nuts. Place on preheated buttered grill and sauté on open grill for 3 minutes. Fill cavity with mint or currant jelly. Serve hot as a meat accompaniment.

spring a tempting surprise with fruit kabobs

SAVORY FRUIT KABOBS
6 servings

6 peaches, cut in half   1 cup pineapple juice
2 bananas, cut into cubes   2 tablespoons Cointreau, optional
2 apples, unpared, cut in wedges   ½ cup honey
1 fresh pineapple, cut in cubes   ½ teaspoon chopped mint
1 grapefruit, sectioned   Melted butter or margarine

1 To prepare the marinade. Combine: fruit juice, Cointreau, honey and mint. Allow fruits to stand in marinade for 30 minutes.

2 Turn dial to 3 or M and preheat grill.

3 String fruit, alternating them on 6 metal skewers. Brush grill with melted fat. Grill kabobs on preheated open grill for 5 to 8 minutes or until fruits are lightly brown. Baste with marinade during grilling and as kabobs are turned. Serve very hot.

Other fruits suited to grilling are cooked prunes, ripe cherries, apricot halves and dates. Seeds are removed, of course. As a novel touch add melon pickles and melon balls.

7 *super sandwiches and quick breads*

Thirty million Americans can't be wrong. That many Americans eat sandwiches daily. The kinds and the times they eat are subject to human caprice. So, the varieties are unlimited, the occasions are many: lunch, supper, between meals, TV parties, bridge clubs and other round-the-clock treats. How else can we dress up left-overs as appealingly? How else can we achieve so much variety in quick, easy and inexpensive meals?

GOOD SANDWICHES IN DOUBLE-QUICK TIME

Sandwiches grilled and toasted to the king's taste are made in a jiffy. Fillings may be prepared in advance and stored in the re-frigerator until wanted. The following are some milestones on the way to sandwich success: use good sliced white or brown bread, corn bread, rolls, etc. For soft golden toast, use fresh bread. Turn dial to highest heat. Spread bread with butter before toasting. For crisp, brown toast, use fresh bread and turn dial to slower heat. Spread bread with butter before toasting. For dark, crunchy toast, use day-old bread, slow heat, no butter. *The spread*. Remove the butter or filling from the refrigerator an hour before using. Spread to the edge as it keeps the filling from soaking through the crisp toast. *The filling*. Be liberal! Allow 3 tablespoons per filling. Several slices of meat or cheese cut thin are better for sandwiches than thick ones. *Serving*. Keep fresh by assembling at the last minute. Serve hot!

GRILLED FAVORITES

The "All-American" well-browned, grilled sandwich is especially practical when served with crisp vegetables and a tossed green salad. Sliced bread, rolls and buns are equally good for grilling. The choice is a matter of preference. Cheese melts perfectly on the grill and is an ideal ingredient. Its golden color, pleasing texture, excellent flavor and food value can hardly be excelled. Several recipes and suggestions follow.

GRILLED CHEESE
4 sandwiches

8 slices bread	Sliced pickles
4 tablespoons butter or margarine	Olives
4 slices Cheddar cheese	Potato chips

1 Turn dial to 3 or M and preheat grill.
2 Remove crusts from bread, if desired. Brush one side of each slice with softened butter or margarine.
3 Place slices of cheese between unbuttered sides of bread.
4 Cook in closed grill until toast is golden brown, usually about 4 minutes. Serve very hot with desired garnishes and accompaniments.

CORNED BEEFBURGERS
2 sandwiches

Preheat grill at 3 or M. Combine and mix well ½ cup minced canned or cooked corned beef, 2 tablespons ketchup, 1 tablespoon minced onion. Use as filling for cut halves of 2 buns. Top with filling. Brush buns with softened butter, toast in closed preheated grill for 4 minutes or until thoroughly heated and lightly browned. Garnish: Onion rings.

GRILLED HAM AND CHEESE
4 sandwiches

Preheat grill at 3 or M. Toast 8 slices bread on one side only. On each toasted side of 4 slices place: 1 slice ham, 1 slice cheese, 1 tablespoon chili sauce. Cover with second slice, toasted side down. Brush untoasted outer slices with softened butter or margarine. Toast in closed, preheated grill about 4 minutes or until golden brown. Garnish: pickles.

GRILLED PARTY SANDWICHES
6 sandwiches

Preheat grill at 3 or M. Sauté ½ cup sliced mushrooms, ⅓ cup sliced olives, and 1 tablespoon minced onion in 2 tablespoons butter or margarine. Toast 12 slices bread on one side only. Spread mushroom-olive mixture on 6 toasted sides, top with 6 cheese slices, cover with second slice, toasted side down. Brush untoasted sides of sandwiches with soft butter, toast in closed, preheated grill, for about 4 minutes or until golden brown.

GRILLED FRANKFURTER-CHEESE BUNS
6 sandwiches

Preheat grill at 3 or M. Cut ¼ pound sharp Cheddar cheese in ½ inch strips long enough to stuff 6 frankfurters which have been slashed down the center almost end to end. Wrap with slices of bacon, secure with toothpicks. Brown in closed, preheated grill until bacon is crisp. Buns may be sliced and toasted at the same time; all will be done in about 4 minutes. Serve hot with pickle relish.

BACON WRAPPED cheese-stuffed frankfurters may be prepared in advance and stored in the refrigerator until ready to be grilled. This is especially popular with the high school crowd.

HAM SAVORY
6 servings

Preheat grill at 3 or M. Combine and mix well 1 cup cooked, chopped ham, ⅓ cup salad dressing and ½ teaspoon salt. Place on 6 pieces of light, brown toast and grill on preheated open grill.

PEANUT BUTTER AND BACON
6 servings

Preheat grill at 3 or M. Combine and mix well ⅔ cup peanut butter, ¼ cup salad dressing, 2 tablespoons pickle relish, 4 tablespoons cooked bacon bits. Place on 6 pieces of toast. Grill on preheated open grill.

CHEESE TOAST WITH SHRIMP SALAD

6 servings

Preheat grill at 3 or M. Combine and mix well 1½ cups cooked, chopped shrimp, ⅓ cup chopped celery and ¼ cup salad dressing. Reserve to place on 6 lettuce leaves. Cover 6 slices of lightly toasted bread with 6 slices of sharp cheese. Melt cheese on preheated open grill. Serve: salad in lettuce leaves on top of grilled cheese toast. Delicious!

BACON-CHEESE-TOMATO COMBINATION

4 servings

Preheat grill at 3 or M. Toast 4 slices of bread on one side. On each slice place 1 teaspoon mayonnaise dressing, spread to edge. Add 2 tomato slices and 1 thick slice sharp cheese. Top with partially cooked slices of bacon. Grill on closed grill until bacon is well done.

LUNCHEON SANDWICHES

6 servings

Preheat grill at 3 or M. Combine and mix well 1 cup chopped shrimp (or flaked crab or tuna), 2 chopped hard-cooked eggs, ¼ cup undiluted cream of mushroom soup, and 2 tablespoons pimiento strips. Place on 6 pieces lightly browned toast. Grill on preheated open grill.

LEFT-OVER fish, poultry or meat may be used successfully. Minced celery may be used either with or instead of the chopped hard-cooked eggs. Cheese sauce may be used instead of the cream of mushroom soup. This grilled specialty lends itself to your imagination.

3-DECKER CLUB SANDWICHES

These sandwiches are especially popular for lunch or supper since they are hearty enough to satisfy anyone and appetizing enough to tempt every palate. Fillings are according to personal preferences. Here are some of the most popular combinations but with culinary imagination you can create new ones.

Sliced tongue, ham, roast beef, cheese, sautéed Canadian bacon, crisp bacon slices, crab salad, egg salad, cole slaw, and pickles are interesting filling possibilities.

CHICKEN CLUB
1 sandwich

3 slices bread	2 slices cooked chicken
Butter or margarine	2 crisp slices bacon
Salad dressing	2 slices tomato
Lettuce	Garnishes

1 Turn dial to 3 or M and preheat grill.
2 Toast bread on grill. Brush one side of toast with butter or margarine.
3 First layer: Cover buttered side with chicken, spread lightly with salad dressing, top with lettuce. Cover with second piece of toast, buttered side up.
4 Second layer: Spread buttered toast with salad dressing. Cover with slices of tomato and grilled bacon. Top with third piece of toast, buttered side down.
5 Secure each corner with a toothpick. Cut diagonally into halves or quarters. Place upright on a plate. Serve immediately while toast is crisp. Garnish with pickles, olives, radishes or potato chips.

A SANDWICH BAR

Party-wise hostesses delight in serving their guests with as little formality as possible. Some with a flair for the new and unusual are happily solving the service problem by setting up a sandwich bar, indoors or out.

The basic idea of the sandwich bar is to offer guests the tempting wherewithal to make, grill or toast their own sandwiches. Needless to say, this gives them the opportunity to be creative while catering to their own tastes.

Simplicity is the keynote for a successful sandwich bar. Do not confuse guests with too lavish a choice of breads and fillings. And have someone 'man' the grill to guide the guests in toasting or grilling their creations.

Besides the grill, breads and fillings, a well set-up bar should have a bowl each of softened butter and salad dressing with spatulas or spreaders for fillings and spreads. Don't forget salt and pepper and a tray with sliced tomatoes, lettuce and relishes.

EASY-TO-MAKE FILLINGS

Here are some suggestions for fillings for grilled and toasted sandwiches which should be prepared well in advance and refrigerated until needed. 1 cup of filling is recommended for 6 sandwiches and 3 tablespoons for 1 sandwich. Spread generously to edges of the bread.

EGG-HAM

Combine and mix well: 2 hard-cooked chopped eggs, ½ cup canned deviled ham, 1 tablespoon A-1 sauce, 2 tablespoons minced onion.

PEANUT BUTTER-BACON

Combine and mix well: ½ cup peanut butter, ½ cup chili sauce, ½ cup cooked chopped crisp bacon.

EGG SALAD

Combine and mix well: 3 hard-cooked chopped eggs, ¼ cup chopped olives, 2 tablespoons salad dressing.

DRIED BEEF-CHEESE

Combine and mix well: ¾ cup chopped dried beef, ½ cup grated processed cheese, ¼ cup salad dressing, ¼ cup chopped celery.

SALAMI-EGG SALAD

Combine and mix well: ½ cup chopped salami (¼ pound), 2 tablespoons pickle relish, 2 tablespoons chopped celery, 2 tablespoons salad dressing, 1 hard-cooked chopped egg.

TUNA TOPPING

Combine and mix well: 1 can (7-ounces) flaked, drained tuna, 2 tablespoons minced onion, 2 tablespoons chopped pickle and 2 tablespoons salad dressing. (Excellent grilled for open-faced sandwiches.)

it's magic how the sticks disappear into thin air

MAGIC BREAD STICKS

24 sticks

1 unsliced loaf (8-inch)   Melted butter or margarine

1 Turn dial to 3 or M and preheat grill.
2 Trim crusts from loaf of bread. Cut lengthwise into 1 inch thick slices and then cut each long slice into 3 sticks, crosswise. Brush each with melted butter or margarine on all sides.
3 Place on preheated grill. Toast on closed grill for 2 minutes or until golden brown; or on an open grill until brown, turn and toast an additional 2 minutes.

GARLIC BUTTER. Brush bread with mixture of ½ cup melted butter and ¼ teaspoon garlic power or crushed garlic cloves to taste.

HERB BUTTER. Add 1 teaspoon dried parsley, ½ teaspoon thyme and ½ teaspoon marjoram to ½ cup melted butter.

an eye-opener for breakfast from left-over bread

FRENCH TOAST

6 servings

3 eggs   ¼ cup milk
½ teaspoon salt   6 slices day old bread
1 tablespoon sugar   Butter or margarine

1 Turn dial to 3 or M and preheat grill.
2 Combine eggs, salt, sugar and milk. Dip bread in egg-milk mixture. Dip quickly for firm toast; dip slowly for soft toast.
3 Brush grill with butter or margarine. Place French toast on heated greased grill, close grill, and brown for 3 minutes. Or toast on open grill for 3 minutes, turn and brown other side. Serve hot.

WAFFLED FRENCH TOAST. Place prepared French toast on preheated waffle grid, close and bake for 2 minutes or until browned. Serve hot.

an attractive and satisfying luncheon or supper dish

CHEESE FRENCH TOAST
6 servings

6 slices whole wheat bread
3 tablespoons butter or margarine
3 slices American cheese, 4 x 4 inches

3 eggs
¼ cup milk
¼ teaspoon salt
Butter or margarine for the grill

1 Turn dial to 3 or M and preheat grill.
2 Prepare sandwiches by removing crusts and buttering slices lightly. Place cheese between slices of bread. Cut sandwiches in half, fasten with toothpicks.
3 Beat eggs slightly. Stir in milk and salt. Use this as a dip for sandwiches.
4 Brush preheated grill generously with butter. Place sandwiches on open grill and brown for 5 minutes. Turn, brown other side. Serve hot.

TOAST
4 servings

4 slices day old bread   Butter or margarine

1 Turn dial to 4 or past M and preheat grill.
2 Toast bread slices in closed grill for 3 minutes or until done.
3 Serve hot with butter or margarine.

WAFFLE CINNAMON TOAST. Prepare slices of bread. Butter one side and sprinkle with mixture of 3 tablespoons sugar to ¾ teaspoon cinnamon. Place in preheated waffle grid, close and brown. Serve hot.

TOASTED DOUGHNUTS. Turn dial to 3 or M and preheat grill. Cut doughnuts in half. Dot cut surface with butter. Place in closed grill for 2 or 3 minutes until lightly browned. Serve hot.

TOASTED POUND CAKE. Turn dial to 3 or M and preheat grill. Slice day old cake 1 inch thick. Butter both sides generously. Dip buttered slices in maple syrup, honey or mixture of 3 tablespoons sugar to ¾ teaspoon cinnamon; roll in chopped nuts or coconut. Toast cake slices on open or closed grill 2-3 minutes until lightly browned. Serve hot.

everybody enjoys cinnamon toast served with apple sauce

CINNAMON TOAST
8 servings

8 slices bread	¼ cup sugar
¼ cup melted butter	1 teaspoon cinnamon

1 Turn dial to 4 or past M and preheat grill.
2 Trim crusts from bread, cut slices in half. Brush both sides of bread with melted butter. Combine sugar and cinnamon. Dip each piece of buttered toast in mixture.
3 Toast on open or closed grill 1 to 2 minutes or until golden brown. Serve hot.

ORANGE TOAST. Omit cinnamon. Add ¼ teaspoon grated orange rind and 1 tablespoon orange juice to sugar. Toast as directed.

MAPLE TOAST. Omit cinnamon. Use maple sugar instead of white sugar. Toast as directed.

8 *fluffy pancakes to melt in your mouth*

Mouth-watering, fluffy, tender, delicately-browned pancakes have rated many a hostess as an expert. By mastering a few tricks, anyone can make pancakes at a moment's notice, using only the simple ingredients found in every kitchen.

In all lands and in every age, cakes of meal and water were baked on heated stones or primitive stoves. The soldiers of ancient Greece and Rome flapped pancakes. In the Middle Ages pancakes acquired a religious significance and their ingredients were symbolic: flour for the staff of life, milk for innocence, salt for wholesomeness and eggs as desirable food.

Pancakes have taken on various guises with slight changes here and there. *Hot Cakes or Stacks of Wheat* are prepared from a batter of flour, milk and little or no egg. *Griddlecakes* are prepared from batter as for hot cakes but with more egg, so they are tender, large and fluffy. *Pancakes* are prepared from batter as for hot cakes but with more egg. They are usually made into thin cakes suitable for roll-up and for desserts. *Flap-jacks* are prepared from griddle-cake batter sturdy enough to "flap."

INGREDIENTS

Pancakes are prepared with the same ingredients as waffles: all-purpose flour, sugar, baking powder, shortening, eggs and milk with additions such as coconut, spices, dates, chocolate, chopped nuts, cheese and others which change flavor, texture and color.

PREPARATION

Equipment. Minimum is two mixing bowls, a beater, measuring cups and spoons, mixing spoon, ladle. Even less equipment is needed with a quick mix.

DRY INGREDIENTS. Measure and sift thoroughly sifted flour, salt, baking powder and sugar.

LIQUID INGREDIENTS. Measure and mix eggs, milk and melted fat as directed in the recipe—the methods vary.

COMBINING INGREDIENTS. Stir only to blend. If egg whites are to be folded in last, handle very carefully. The thin batter is now ready to be ladled onto the preheated griddle.

SUCCESS POINTERS

TO MAKE THE BATTER. Do use a reliable recipe or mix; do measure ingredients carefully; do sift dry ingredients together thoroughly; do combine the egg, milk and melted fat until well blended; do stir the batter very gently until just mixed. The little lumps disappear in baking. Overmixing will produce a tough pancake.

TO STORE THE BATTER. Store covered in the refrigerator for a day or so.

TO BAKE THE BATTER. Do read the manufacturer's directions about preheating. Medium heat or the center of your dial is correct, but some griddles may require higher than medium. Do test the griddle by sprinkling on a few drops of water to see if they dance merrily and evaporate. Try a teaspoon of batter to see if it sizzles as it bakes. Do make sure of round, perfect pancakes by ladling the batter in one, quick motion close to the griddle. Spooning batter makes unevenly shaped pancakes. Do watch the baking time— about 2 minutes. When pancakes are bubbly and edges dry, loosen with a spatula, turn once. The other side bakes in about 1 minute. Do not pat. Do not overcrowd griddle. Bake only as many as you can watch and turn. Do use a salt bag to pick up bits of browned batter if pancakes stick. It is much better than greasing. To prepare a salt bag, place 1 cup of salt in the center of a square cotton cloth. Tie well with string. To eliminate possible sticking troubles, use after baking each batch. Bake cakes only as needed.

TO SERVE THE CAKES. Serve quickly on heated plates or keep covered in skillet (with cover at an angle to allow steam to escape) or keep warm in oven (300° F.) 3 deep and covered with towel.

Perfectly round pancakes baked in the size you and your family prefer are easy to make if you use the following measures:

3-inch pancakes require ¼ cup measure as ladle
4-inch pancakes require a scant 1/3 cup measure as ladle
5-inch pancakes require 1/3 cup measure as ladle
8-inch pancakes require ¾ cup measure as ladle
Dollar size dessert pancakes, use tablespoon as ladle

PANCAKES FROM QUICK MIXES

Quick mixes insure excellent results if directions are closely followed. They cost about half and the preparation time is less than one third compared to homemade pancakes. Variations are the same as for standard recipes. The average package will make about 30 pancakes. However, if a package is opened and only a part used, closely seal the remainder to prevent loss of flavor. Prepared mixes are ideal for a number of people, for two persons, or for you only, if you live alone. Any of the pancake quick mixes may be varied with the following additions.

HOW TO VARY PANCAKE BATTER

BLUEBERRY. Add ½ cup thawed frozen blueberries before baking.

CORN. Add 1 cup drained, cooked or canned corn before baking.

HAM. Add 1 cup finely chopped ham before baking.

PINEAPPLE. Add ½ cup drained, crushed pineapple before baking.

"mighty good", and no mistake

"MIGHTY GOOD" PANCAKES
24 5-inch or 12 8-inch pancakes

2 cups sifted all-purpose flour
3 teaspoons baking powder
½ teaspoon salt
1 tablespoon sugar

2 eggs
2 cups milk
3 tablespoons melted fat

1   Turn dial to 3 or M and preheat griddle.
2   Sift together flour, baking powder, salt and sugar into a mixing bowl.
3   Beat eggs until light. Add milk and melted fat. Mix well.
4   Gradually add egg-milk-fat mixture to dry sifted ingredients. Do not overmix. Batter will be lumpy.
5   Test griddle. Ladle each pancake with a 1 cup measure. Pour with a single, quick motion. (Use ½ cup measure for 5-inch pancakes, the ¾ cup measure for 8-inch pancakes.) Bake for 2 minutes or until pancake is bubbly and golden brown. Turn with a spatula and bake 1 minute more.

RICH GOLDEN PANCAKES
8 4-inch pancakes

1 cup sifted all-purpose flour	1 egg
3 teaspoons baking powder	1 cup milk
1 teaspoon sugar	¼ cup sour cream
¼ teaspoon salt	2 tablespoons melted fat

1 Turn dial to 3 or M and preheat griddle.
2 Sift together flour, baking powder, sugar and salt into a mixing bowl.
3 Beat egg until light. Add milk, cream and melted fat. Mix well.
4 Gradually add egg-milk-fat mixture to sifted dry ingredients. Do not overmix. Batter will be lumpy.
5 Test griddle. Ladle each pancake with ¼ cup measure. Pour with a single, quick motion. Bake 2 minutes or until pancake is bubbly and golden brown. Turn with a spatula and bake 1 minute more.

FEATHERWEIGHT PANCAKES
12 4-inch pancakes

¼ cup sifted all-purpose flour	3 eggs, separated
¼ teaspoon salt	¾ cup cottage cheese

1 Turn dial to 3 or M and preheat griddle.
2 Sift together flour and salt into a mixing bowl.
3 Beat egg whites until stiff and reserve to fold in last. Beat yolks until light.
4 Gradually add flour and cottage cheese. Carefully fold in stiffly beaten egg whites. Do not overmix. Batter will be lumpy.
5 Test griddle. Ladle each pancake with a ¼ cup measure. Pour with a single, quick motion. Bake 2 minutes or until pancake is bubbly and golden brown. Turn. Bake 1 minute more.

fluffy and irresistible

FLUFFY BUTTERMILK PANCAKES
16 4-inch pancakes

1½ cups sifted all-purpose flour	½ teaspoon salt
1 teaspoon baking powder	3 eggs, separated
1 teaspoon baking soda	1⅔ cups thick buttermilk
2 tablespoons sugar	3 tablespoons melted fat

1 Turn dial to 3 or M and preheat griddle.
2 Sift together flour, baking powder, soda, sugar and salt.
3 Beat egg whites until stiff and reserve to fold in last. Beat egg yolks until light. Add buttermilk and melted fat. Mix well.
4 Gradually add egg-milk-fat mixture to sifted dry ingredients. Stir just enough to moisten dry ingredients. Carefully fold in stiffly beaten egg whites.
5 Test griddle. Ladle each pancake with a ¼ cup measure. Pour with a single, quick motion. Bake 2 minutes or until pancake is bubbly and golden brown. Turn with a spatula and bake 1 minute more.

Dutch housewives introduced this favorite in 1617

BUCKWHEAT PANCAKES
8 5-inch pancakes

1 cup buckwheat flour	1 teaspoon salt
1 cup sifted all-purpose flour	1 egg
4 teaspoons baking powder	2¼ cups milk
1 tablespoon sugar	¼ cup melted fat

1 Turn dial to 3 or M to preheat griddle.
2 Sift together buckwheat flour, flour, baking powder, sugar and salt into a mixing bowl.

3   Beat egg until light, add milk and melted fat. Mix well.
4   Gradually pour egg-milk-fat mixture into dry ingredients. Stir
    with as few strokes as possible to blend. Do not overmix.
5   Test griddle. Use a ¼ cup measure as a ladle, pour with a single,
    quick motion. Bake 2 minutes or until pancake is bubbly and
    golden brown. Turn with a spatula and bake 1 minute more.

all-time all-American favorite

STACK OF WHEATS
20 3-inch pancakes

2 cups wholewheat flour	1 egg
4 teaspoons baking powder	2½ cups milk
1 tablespoon sugar	3 tablespoons melted fat
1 teaspoon salt	

1   Turn dial to 3 or M and preheat griddle.
2   Mix thoroughly wholewheat flour, baking powder, sugar and
    salt in a mixing bowl.
3   Beat egg until light, add milk and melted fat. Mix well.
4   Gradually add egg-milk-fat mixture to mixed dry ingredients.
    Do not over mix. Batter will be lumpy.
5   Test griddle. Ladle each pancake with a scant ¼ cup measure.
    Pour with a single, quick motion. Bake 2 minutes or until pan-
    cake is bubbly and golden brown. Turn with a spatula and bake
    1 minute more.

Wholewheat flour is always measured unsifted. Many prefer to
use a blend of both wholewheat and all-purpose flour. If so, sift
the dry ingredients with the all-purpose flour before blending the
two flours.

universal appeal, constant demand

APPLE PANCAKES
16 4-inch pancakes

1 cup raw unpared apple, finely
  chopped
2 tablespoons sugar (for apples)
1½ cups sifted all-purpose flour
3½ teaspoons baking powder
¾ teaspoon salt

3 teaspoons sugar
⅛ teaspoon cinnamon
1 egg
1 cup milk
3 tablespoons melted fat

1 ADVANCE PREPARATION: Sprinkle chopped apple with sugar and
  reserve to fold in last.
2 Turn dial to 3 or M and preheat griddle.
3 Sift together flour, baking powder, salt, sugar and cinnamon
  into a mixing bowl.
4 Beat egg until light. Add milk and melted fat. Mix well.
5 Gradually add egg-milk-fat mixture to sifted dry ingredients.
  Do not overmix. Batter will be lumpy. Fold in chopped apple
  with as few strokes as possible.
6 Test griddle. Ladle each pancake with a ¼ cup measure. Pour
  with a single, quick motion. Bake 2 minutes or until pancake
  is bubbly and golden brown. Turn with a spatula and bake
  1 minute more.

a gay disguise for left-over bread crumbs

CRUMB GRIDDLECAKES
20 3-inch griddlecakes

1½ cups hot milk
2 tablespoons butter or margarine
1½ cups fine bread crumbs
½ cup sifted all-purpose flour

4 teaspoons baking powder
¼ teaspoon salt
2 eggs

1 Turn dial to 3 or M and preheat griddle.
2 Combine milk and butter, stir until blended. Add crumbs. Allow to stand until soft or about 20 minutes.
3 Sift together flour, baking powder and salt into a mixing bowl.
4 Beat eggs until light. Add milk-crumb mixture and combine thoroughly.
5 Gradually add this mixture to sifted dry ingredients. Stir only until well blended.
6 Test griddle. Ladle each griddlecake with a ¼ cup measure. Pour with a single, quick motion. Bake 2 minutes or until griddlecake is bubbly and golden brown. Turn with a spatula and bake 1 minute more.

a Dixie favorite

CORNMEAL GRIDDLECAKES
20 3-inch cakes

1 cup sifted all-purpose flour	2 eggs, separated
1 teaspoon baking soda	2 cups buttermilk
1½ teaspoons salt	3 tablespoons melted fat
1 cup cornmeal	

1 Turn dial to 3 or M and preheat griddle.
2 Sift together flour, soda and salt into a mixing bowl. Stir in cornmeal until well blended.
3 Beat egg whites until stiff and reserve to fold in last. Beat egg yolks, add buttermilk. Mix well.
4 Gradually add egg-buttermilk mixture to sifted dry ingredients. Do not overmix. Batter will be lumpy. Blend in melted fat and carefully fold in stiffly beaten egg whites.
5 Test griddle. Ladle each pancake with a ¼ cup measure. Pour with a single, quick motion. Bake 2 minutes or until pancake is bubbly and golden brown. Turn with a spatula and bake 1 minute more.

frozen or fresh blueberries may be used for this regional favorite

NEW ENGLAND BLUEBERRY PANCAKES

20 4-inch pancakes

2 cups sifted all-purpose flour	2 eggs
3 teaspoons baking powder	1½ cups milk
1 tablespoon sugar	4 tablespoons melted fat
1 teaspoon salt	1 cup well-drained blueberries

1 Turn dial to 3 or M and preheat griddle.
2 Sift together flour, baking powder, sugar and salt into a mixing bowl.
3 Beat eggs until light. Add milk and melted fat. Mix well.
4 Gradually add egg-milk-fat mixture to sifted dry ingredients. Stir just to moisten dry ingredients. Fold in blueberries with as few strokes as possible.
5 Test griddle. Ladle each pancake with a ¼ cup measure. Pour with a single, quick motion. Bake 2 minutes or until pancake is bubbly and golden brown. Turn with a spatula and bake 1 minute more.

BLUEBERRIES may be sprinkled on unbaked pancake batter just before the pancakes are turned to bake the other side. One-half tablespoon blueberries is about the right amount.

an appetizing use for left-over rice

RICE PANCAKES

24 3-inch pancakes

½ cup sifted all-purpose flour	1 cup milk
2 teaspoons baking powder	1 cup cooked rice
½ teaspoon salt	2 tablespoons melted fat
2 eggs, separated	

1 Turn dial to 3 or M and preheat griddle.
2 Sift together flour, baking powder and salt into a mixing bowl.
3 Beat egg whites until stiff and reserve to fold in last. Beat egg yolks, add milk and cooked rice. Mix well.
4 Gradually add egg-milk-rice mixture to sifted dry ingredients. Do not overmix. Batter will be lumpy. Blend in melted fat and carefully fold in stiffly beaten egg whites.
5 Test griddle. Ladle each pancake with a ¼ cup measure. Pour with a single, quick motion. Bake 2 minutes or until pancake is bubbly and golden brown. Turn with a spatula and bake 1 minute more.

APPLE-FILLED POLISH PANCAKES
6 generous servings

Filling:
3 cups apple, cut in julienne strips
½ teaspoon cinnamon
¼ cup sugar

⅓ cup sugar
⅓ cup fine bread crumbs

Pancakes: (6 8-inch)
Favorite recipe

Topping:
⅓ cup melted butter or margarine

1 ADVANCE PREPARATION: Sprinkle apple strips with cinnamon-sugar mixture. Allow apples to stand at least 15 minutes before using to absorb spicy sweetness.
2 Turn dial to 3 or M and preheat.
3 Prepare pancakes as directed in recipe or heat if frozen. Fill center of prepared pancakes with apple strips and roll with care.
4 Place filled pancakes in a buttered baking pan, dot with melted butter. Sprinkle generously with sugar-bread crumb mixture. Bake in a moderate oven (350° F) about 20 minutes or until pancakes are a delicate brown. Serve hot.

an eye-opener for breakfast

PINEAPPLE PANCAKES
12 4-inch pancakes

1¼ cups sifted all-purpose flour
3 teaspoons baking powder
1 tablespoon sugar
½ teaspoon salt
1 egg

1 cup milk
2 tablespoons melted fat
½ cup crushed, canned pineapple, drained

1 Turn dial to 3 or M and preheat griddle.
2 Sift together flour, baking powder, sugar and salt into a mixing bowl.
3 Beat egg until light. Add milk and fat. Mix well.
4 Gradually add egg-milk-fat mixture to sifted dry ingredients. Stir with as few strokes as possible, fold in pineapple. Do not overmix. Batter will be lumpy.
5 Test griddle. Ladle each pancake with a ¼ cup measure. Pour with a single, quick motion. Bake 2 minutes or until pancake is bubbly and golden brown. Turn with a spatula and bake 1 minute more.

for "ahs!" and "oh's" serve these

PANCAKES WITH HAM SAUCE
4 servings

1 pound ham, cut in finger strips
4 tablespoons butter or margarine
½ cup honey
2 tablespoons brown sugar
1 tablespoon prepared mustard

Juice from 2 oranges
Grated rind from 1 orange

Pancakes:
12 5-inch pancakes
Favorite recipe

1 In a saucepan sauté ham strips in butter until slightly browned. Add honey, brown sugar, mustard, orange juice and grated orange rind. Cook for 10 minutes or until thick.

2 Prepare pancakes as described in recipe.

3 Spoon heated ham sauce over tops of hot pancakes. Or stack them layer cake style or serve as filled roll-ups.

9 *waffles are really wonderful*

Golden brown, light, tender and crisp hot waffles add magic to a meal. How very easy it is to prepare and serve them with a modern electric waffle baker.

Waffles were popular in the days of ancient Greece and Rome. Museums display molds with the initials of the bride and groom entwined to decorate the top of the waffle which was baked over an open fire with long metal handles to protect the cook from intense heat. Waffle baking has been simplified since the days when Dutch housewives introduced it to this country in 1617!

Waffles are one of our most adaptable foods. At breakfast they help start the day with that "Oh, what a beautiful morning" feeling. Generously topped with creamed left-over meat or poultry, they are also perfect for a quick meal. On cold wintry or rainy days, waffles "hit the spot." Impromptu guest meals can be prepared with only a few ingredients from your kitchen. Dessert waffles with fruits, berries, ice cream or other toppings will establish you as a hostess with a special know-how.

Here are a few factors that contribute to perfect melt-in-your-mouth waffles for every day as well as "show off" for company. The inexperienced waffle maker will find the step-by-step method indicated below easy to follow.

INGREDIENTS

FLOUR. Unless otherwise stated, all-purpose flour is used. However, cake flour is suggested for some dessert waffles.

SUGAR may be added for flavor and to increase brownness.

BAKING POWDER. Double-acting powder is recommended for waffles.

SHORTENING. Melted butter, margarine, fat, or salad oil.

EGGS. Whole or separated, they must be beaten. If whites are beaten separately, they are gently folded in just before baking.

MILK. Experts sometimes warm milk slightly to make it combine more readily with the melted fat and egg.

ADDITIONS. Coconut, spices, dates, chocolate, chopped nuts, cheese and other additions change flavor, texture and color.

PREPARATION

EQUIPMENT. Minimum is two mixing bowls, a beater, measuring cups and spoons, mixing spoon, ladle. Even less equipment is needed with a quick mix.

DRY INGREDIENTS. Measure and sift thoroughly sifted flour, salt, baking powder and sugar.

LIQUID INGREDIENTS. Measure and blend well beaten eggs, milk and melted fat.

COMBINING INGREDIENTS. Stir only to blend. If egg whites are to be folded in last, handle very gently. The thin batter is now ready to be ladled into the preheated waffle baker.

SUCCESS POINTERS

Preheat waffle baker according to manufacturer's directions—usually about 8 minutes. Ladle thin batter into the center of the grid, spread quickly if necessary, close lid quickly. When browned, loosen edge and remove waffle with a fork. How much batter? Sizes, shapes and depth of grids vary in waffle bakers. However, use the following as a working guide: Large square waffles (4 inch), 1⅓ cups of batter. Round waffles, ½ cup of batter. Twin waffles, ¼ cup of batter for each. How to store batter? Keep covered in refrigerator overnight.

LEFT-OVER WAFFLES may be packaged and frozen to be used within three months. Thaw frozen waffles for 10 minutes then toast in a toaster or heat to serving temperature on a griddle.

FIRST AID FOR WAFFLE ACCIDENTS

If you have followed manufacturer's suggestions and have used tested recipes, it may not be necessary to refer to the following: If waffles are spotted and stick to the waffle baker, the baking temperature may be too low. If the fat is less than 3 tablespoons to each cup of flour and the recipe contains few eggs, the batter may stick to the iron. Increase the fat and the heat to solve this problem. If waffles are hard or tough, baking time is too long so increase the heat. If waffles are brown but not crisp, temperature is too high. If waffles separate and are pale, they are undercooked and should be allowed to bake until the signal appears or the steaming stops. If waffles are skimpy, misshapen, or overflow the waffle baker, the batter measurement is inaccurate. Experiment with measures to make waffles in size and shape desired.

WAFFLES FROM MIXES

Waffles may be prepared from many of the pancake quick mixes by adding beaten eggs and melted fat. For calamity-proof waffles, take advantage of prepared waffle and waffle-pancake mixes and note savings in cost and preparation time. An average box will make about 20 waffles. If only a portion of the box is used, closely seal the remainder with Scotch tape to prevent loss of flavor. Waffles for one, for two or a crowd at short notice are at your fingertips.

A quick meal for unexpected guests may be inspired by using a mix for waffles. The topping may be creamed chicken or fish, dried chipped beef, creamed mushrooms or something from the emergency shelf. Or if you prefer, choose a dessert featuring waffles with a topping of ice cream and sauce or fruit.

SUGGESTED ADDITIONS

APRICOT WAFFLES. Add ¾ cup stewed drained apricots (finely diced) to the batter before folding in egg whites.

BACON WAFFLES. Cut lean strips of bacon to fit sections of the waffle baker. Place a strip in each section, close the baker and cook for 1 minute, add the batter and bake as directed.

HAM WAFFLES. Sprinkle 2 tablespoons finely diced ham over each waffle just before baking.

NUT WAFFLES. Sprinkle 1 tablespoon chopped nut meats over each waffle just before baking.

PINEAPPLE WAFFLES. Add 2/3 cup drained crushed pineapple to the batter before folding in the egg whites.

surprise! mmm—so good and no eggs to beat separately

WONDERFUL WAFFLES
8 waffles

2½ cups sifted all-purpose flour   2 eggs
4 tablespoons baking powder   2¼ cups milk
1½ tablespoons sugar   ¼ cup melted fat
1 teaspoon salt

1   Turn dial to 3 or M and preheat waffle baker.
2   Sift together flour, baking powder, sugar and salt into a mixing bowl.
3   Beat eggs until light, add milk and melted fat. Mix well.
4   Gradually add egg-milk-fat mixture to sifted dry ingredients. Stir with as few strokes as possible.
5   Ladle batter onto preheated waffle baker. Bake 3 to 4 minutes until steaming stops.
6   Let waffle baker heat before pouring batter for the next waffle.

old-fashioned crisp waffles—a favorite for generations

BUTTERMILK WAFFLES
8 waffles

2 cups sifted all-purpose flour   2 eggs
2 teaspoons baking powder   2 cups buttermilk
½ teaspoon baking soda   6 tablespoons melted fat
½ teaspoon salt

1   Turn dial to 3 or M and preheat waffle baker.
2   Sift together flour, baking powder, baking soda and salt.
3   Beat eggs until light, add buttermilk and melted fat. Mix well.
4   Gradually add sifted dry ingredients to egg-milk-fat mixture. Stir carefully with as few strokes as possible.
5   Ladle batter onto preheated waffle baker. Bake 3 to 4 minutes until steaming stops.
6   Let waffle baker heat before pouring next waffle.

waffles in a hurry to prepare in advance, cover and refrigerate

REFRIGERATOR WAFFLES
8 waffles

2 cups sifted all-purpose flour	2 eggs, separated
3 teaspoons baking powder	2 cups milk
1 teaspoon salt	½ cup melted fat

1 Turn dial to 3 or M and preheat waffle baker.
2 Sift together flour, baking powder and salt into a mixing bowl.
3 Beat egg whites until stiff and reserve to fold in last. Beat egg yolks until light, add milk and fat. Mix well.
4 Gradually add egg-milk mixture to sifted dry ingredients. Stir with as few strokes as possible. Carefully fold in stiffly beaten egg whites.
5 Ladle batter onto preheated waffle baker. Bake 3 to 4 minutes until steaming stops.
6 Let waffle baker heat before pouring batter for next waffle.

old-fashioned treat for waffle enthusiasts

GRANDMA'S SUNDAY WAFFLES
6 waffles

1½ cups sifted all-purpose flour	2 eggs, separated
1 teaspoon baking powder	1 cup milk
½ teaspoon salt	¼ cup melted butter

1 Turn dial to 3 or M and preheat waffle baker.
2 Sift together flour, baking powder and salt.
3 Beat egg whites until stiff and reserve to fold in last. Beat egg yolks until light, add alternately milk and sifted dry ingredients, stir in melted butter with as few strokes as possible. Carefully fold in stiffly beaten egg whites.
4 Ladle batter onto preheated waffle baker. Bake 3 to 4 minutes until steaming stops.
5 Let waffle baker heat before pouring batter for next waffle.

count on second and third helpings with this one

LARGE SQUARE WAFFLES
5 whoppers—20 sections

4 cups sifted cake flour
6 teaspoons baking powder
2 teaspoons salt
2 tablespoons sugar

4 eggs, separated
2½ cups milk
¾ cup melted fat

1 Turn dial to 3 or M and preheat waffle baker.
2 Sift together flour, baking powder, salt and sugar.
3 Beat egg whites until stiff and reserve to fold in last. Beat egg yolks until light.
4 Add milk and sifted dry ingredients alternately and stir with as few strokes as possible. Stir in melted fat. Blend. Carefully fold in stiffly beaten egg whites.
5 Ladle batter onto preheated waffle baker. Bake 3 to 4 minutes until steaming stops.
6 Let waffle baker heat before pouring batter for next waffle.

just right for a speedy treat for breakfast or lunch

WAFFLES FOR TWO
4 waffles

1⅓ cups sifted all-purpose flour
1 teaspoon baking powder
½ teaspoon salt

1 egg, separated
1 cup milk
3 tablespoons melted fat

1 Turn dial to 3 or M and preheat waffle baker.
2 Sift together flour, baking powder and salt into a mixing bowl.
3 Beat egg white until stiff and reserve to fold in last. Beat egg yolk until light, add milk and melted fat. Mix well.

4   Gradually add egg yolk-milk-fat mixture to sifted dry ingredients. Stir carefully with as few strokes as possible. Fold in stiffly beaten egg white.
5   Ladle batter onto preheated waffle baker. Bake 3 to 4 minutes until steaming stops.
6   Let waffle baker heat before pouring batter for next waffle.

compliments from guests are inevitable

PARTY WAFFLES
8 waffles

2 cups sifted all-purpose flour	4 eggs, separated
3 teaspoons baking powder	1½ cups milk
1 teaspoon salt	½ cup melted fat
2 tablespoons sugar	

1   Turn dial to 3 or M and preheat waffle baker.
2   Sift together flour, baking powder, salt and sugar into a mixing bowl.
3   Beat egg whites until stiff and reserve to fold in last. Beat egg yolks until light, add milk and melted fat. Mix well.
4   Gradually add egg-milk-fat mixture to sifted dry ingredients. Stir with as few strokes as possible. Carefully fold in stiffly beaten egg whites.
5   Ladle batter onto preheated waffle baker. Bake 3 to 4 minutes until steaming stops.
6   Let waffle baker heat before pouring batter for next waffle.

FEATURE SEVERAL ACCOMPANIMENTS such as honey, maple syrup, strawberry jam and plenty of melted butter. Crisp bacon strips or sausages will complete the temptation that no one will wish to resist.

success guaranteed every time

COCONUT WAFFLES
8 waffles

2½ cups sifted all-purpose flour
4 teaspoons baking powder
1 teaspoon salt
2 eggs, separated

2 cups milk
¼ cup melted fat
1½ cups shredded coconut

1 Turn dial to 3 or M and preheat waffle baker.
2 Sift flour, baking powder and salt into a mixing bowl.
3 Beat egg whites until stiff and reserve to fold in last. Beat egg yolks until light, add milk. Mix well.
4 Gradually add egg yolk-milk mixture to sifted dry ingredients. Stir with as few strokes as possible. Add fat and coconut, blend into batter. Carefully fold in stiffly beaten egg whites.
5 Ladle batter onto preheated waffle baker. Bake 3 to 4 minutes until steaming stops.
6 Let waffle baker heat before pouring batter for next waffle.

SPRINKLE SNIPPED COCONUT on top of the unbaked plain waffle if you prefer. Bake the waffles as directed. To snip coconut, cut with scissors.

for Sunday brunch or as a waffle base for creamed foods

CHEESE WAFFLES
12 waffles

2 cups sifted all-purpose flour
4 teaspoons baking powder
2 tablespoons sugar
1 teaspoon salt
3 eggs, separated

2 cups milk
½ pound shredded Cheddar cheese
½ cup melted fat

1 Turn dial to 3 or M and preheat waffle baker.
2 Sift together flour, baking powder, sugar and salt into a mixing bowl.
3 Beat egg whites until stiff and reserve to fold in last. Beat egg yolks until light, add milk and cheese. Mix well.
4 Add egg-yolk-milk-cheese mixture to sifted dry ingredients with as few strokes as possible. Stir in melted fat. Carefully fold in stiffly beaten egg whites.
5 Ladle batter onto preheated waffle baker. Bake 3 to 4 minutes until steaming stops.
6 Let waffle baker heat before pouring batter for next waffle.

looking for a very tender, delectable waffle? this is it

SOUR CREAM WAFFLES
8 waffles

1¾ cups sifted all-purpose flour
2 teaspoons baking powder
1 teaspoon baking soda
½ teaspoon salt

3 eggs, separated
2 cups sour cream
½ cup melted fat

1 Turn dial to 3 or M and preheat waffle baker.
2 Sift together flour, baking powder, soda and salt into a mixing bowl.
3 Beat egg whites until stiff and reserve to fold in last. Beat egg yolks, add sour cream. Mix well.
4 Gradually add egg-sour cream mixture to sifted dry ingredients. Stir in melted fat. Carefully fold in stiffly beaten egg whites.
5 Ladle batter onto preheated waffle baker. Bake 3 to 4 minutes until steaming stops.
6 Let waffle baker heat before pouring batter for next waffle.

mark this page—you'll be tempted to use often after first trial

BANANA WAFFLES
6 waffles

1½ cups sifted cake flour
1½ teaspoons baking powder
¾ teaspoon salt
1 tablespoon sugar

2 eggs
¾ cup milk
¼ cup melted fat
1½ cups diced bananas

1   Turn dial to 3 or M and preheat waffle baker.
2   Sift together flour, baking powder, salt and sugar into a mixing bowl.
3   Beat eggs until light. Add milk and melted fat. Mix well.
4   Add egg-milk-fat mixture to sifted dry ingredients. Stir carefully and with as few strokes as possible. Fold in the bananas.
5   Ladle batter onto preheated waffle baker. Spread bananas evenly over the grids. Bake 3 to 4 minutes until steaming stops.
6   Let waffle baker heat before pouring batter for next waffle.

rice waffles originated in the South but are popular everywhere

LOUISIANA RICE WAFFLES
4 waffles

1 cup sifted all-purpose flour
2 teaspoons baking powder
½ teaspoon salt
1 tablespoon sugar

2 eggs, separated
1 cup milk
1 cup cooked cold rice
¼ cup melted fat

1   Turn dial to 3 or M and preheat waffle baker.
2   Sift flour, baking powder, salt and sugar into a mixing bowl.
3   Beat egg whites until stiff and reserve to fold in last. Beat egg yolks until light, add milk. Mix well.

4 Gradually add egg-milk mixture to sifted ingredients. Stir with as few strokes as possible. Add rice, and melted fat. Blend. Do not overmix. Carefully fold in stiffly beaten egg whites.

5 Ladle batter onto preheated waffle baker. Bake 3 to 4 minutes until steaming stops.

6 Let waffle baker heat before pouring next waffle.

homemade treats are so welcome

SYRUPS AND SAUCES FOR WAFFLES

OLD-FASHIONED SOUTHERN SYRUP: Combine 1 cup dark brown sugar (packed), 1/3 cup water and 1 tablespoon sugar. Place on the fire, allow to boil for 2 minutes, stirring constantly. Serve hot.

MAPLE FLAVORED SYRUP: Combine 1 cup light brown sugar (packed) and ½ cup water. Heat to boiling and stir until sugar melts. Add ½ teaspoon maple flavoring and 1 tablespoon butter. Serve hot.

HONEY BUTTER: Combine 1 cup strained honey and ¼ cup butter. Heat to blend; add a dash of cinnamon. Serve hot.

PRALINE SAUCE: Combine 1 cup brown sugar (packed), ½ cup water, ⅛ teaspoon salt. Cook for 5 minutes. Add ½ teaspoon maple flavoring and ½ cup chopped nuts. Serve hot.

CINNAMON SUGAR TOPPING: Combine 1 cup sugar, 2 teaspoons flour, ⅛ teaspoon salt, and ½ teaspoon cinnamon. Add 2/3 cup water. Bring to a boil, cook 3 minutes, stirring constantly. Add 3 tablespoons butter. Serve hot.

ORANGE HONEY SAUCE: Combine ½ cup orange juice, ½ cup honey, and ½ cup diced peeled orange. Heat until blended. Serve hot.

FLUFFY ORANGE SAUCE: Combine ½ cup orange juice, 1 tablespoon grated rind, 1 cup sugar and 1 egg. Cook over low heat until thickened. When cooled and just before serving, fold in 1 cup heavy cream well whipped. Serve immediately.

PINEAPPLE MINT SAUCE FOR WAFFLES: Combine 1 tablespoon cornstarch, ¼ cup sugar, 1 cup crushed pineapple, 1 cup pineapple juice. Cook until clear, stir constantly. Fold in a few bits of chopped mint leaves or a few drops of mint flavoring. Top ice cream with this sauce.

10 *delicious desserts from grill and waffle baker*

Spring a surprise some day with a gay and satisfyingly good dessert that requires only a few minutes to prepare. Serve it in style from your Grill-Waffler, thus dramatizing your specialty before the very eyes of family or guests. Even an amateur psychologist can tell you that "all will be forgiven" if, after an indifferent meal too hastily prepared, the cook comes across with a really good dessert.

Since family and friends look upon the dessert as the fun-part of a meal, try to avoid the monotony of habitually repeating. Every one will agree that few goodies can be as incredibly delectable as freshly baked gingerbread, apple pie, or moist and rich devil's food but not every day, please. Even though a gingerbread waffle topped with chilled apple sauce and cream perhaps meets with enthusiastic approval, a change to strawberry shortcake will be welcomed especially when the shortcake is a dessert waffle with the flavor, texture and brownness exactly right.

In winter the grill and waffle baker is ideal for serving desserts piping hot from the grill or the griddle. In summer it affords relief from sessions in the heated kitchen and an opportunity for a favorite sherbet or ice cream as well as fruits and sauces. A crowning touch would be to invite each person to select a topping from your appealing offerings. Thus the grill and waffle baker makes the preparation of a "yummy" dessert as simple as A B C.

the cook deserves and receives unstinted praise

DATE SPONGE CAKE WAFFLES
4 servings

1 cup sifted cake flour	1½ cups chopped dates
1 teaspoon baking powder	½ cup chopped nuts
½ teaspoon salt	½ cup melted fat
5 eggs, separated	½ teaspoon grated lemon rind
1 cup sugar	

1 Turn dial to 3 or M and preheat waffle baker.

2 Sift together flour, baking powder and salt into a mixing bowl.

3 Beat egg whites until stiff and reserve to fold in last. Beat egg yolks until light. Add sugar gradually and continue beating. Add dates, nuts, melted fat and grated lemon rind to egg-sugar mixture. Mix well.

4 Gradually add egg-date-fat mixture to sifted dry ingredients. Stir with as few strokes as possible. Carefully fold in stiffly beaten egg whites. Do not overmix. Batter will be lumpy.

5 Ladle batter onto preheated waffle baker. Bake 3 to 4 minutes until steaming stops.

6 Let waffle baker heat before pouring batter for next waffle.

DATES AND NUTS may be sprinkled on the top of the unbaked waffle in the waffle baker. This insures a more even distribution. The waffles are baked as directed. Either method produces an excellent waffle.

brownies à la mode—a fitting climax to any meal

BROWNIE NUT WAFFLES
8 waffles

1½ cups sifted all-purpose flour
2 teaspoons baking powder
½ teaspoon salt
1 cup sugar
2 eggs, separated
¾ cup milk

½ cup melted fat
4 squares (4 ozs.) melted
    chocolate
½ cup chopped nuts
1 teaspoon vanilla

1 Turn dial to 3 or M and preheat waffle baker.
2 Sift together flour, baking powder, salt and sugar into a mixing bowl.
3 Beat egg whites until stiff and reserve to fold in last. Beat egg yolks until light, add milk, melted chocolate and fat. Mix well.
4 Gradually add egg-milk-chocolate-fat mixture to dry ingredients. Stir with as few strokes as possible. Blend in nuts and vanilla. Carefully fold in stiffly beaten egg whites. Do not overmix. Batter will be lumpy.
5 Ladle batter onto preheated waffle baker. Bake 3 to 4 minutes until steaming stops.
6 Let waffle baker heat before pouring batter for next waffle.

BROWNIE NUT WAFFLES may be topped with ice cream and a fudge or chocolate sauce for red letter days. One successful hostess allows her guests to top the waffle in the manner they choose. If vanilla ice cream is used the dark sauce seems to dramatize the dessert.

top with ice cream for a special treat

ORANGE NUT WAFFLES

6 waffles

2 cups sifted all-purpose flour	1 cup milk
2 teaspoons baking powder	½ cup orange juice
¾ teaspoon salt	2 tablespoons grated orange rind
2 eggs, separated	½ cup chopped nuts
⅓ cup melted fat	

1 Turn dial to 3 or M and preheat waffle baker.
2 Sift together flour, baking powder and salt into a mixing bowl.
3 Beat egg whites until stiff and reserve to fold in last. Beat egg yolks until light. Add milk, orange juice and rind. Mix well.
4 Gradually add egg-milk-fat-orange mixture to sifted dry ingredients. Combine with as few strokes as possible. Carefully fold in nuts and stiffly beaten egg whites.
5 Ladle batter onto preheated waffle baker. Bake 3 to 4 minutes until steaming stops.
6 Let waffle baker heat before pouring batter for next waffle.

top with chilled apple sauce or ice cream. Exciting!

GINGERBREAD WAFFLES

6 waffles

2 cups sifted all-purpose flour	¼ teaspoon cinnamon
1¼ teaspoons baking soda	2 eggs, separated
2 teaspoons baking powder	1 cup dark molasses
1½ teaspoons ginger	½ cup sour milk
1 teaspoon salt	⅓ cup melted fat

1 Turn dial to 3 or M and preheat waffle baker.
2 Sift together flour, soda, salt, ginger and cinnamon into a mix-

ing bowl. Sift twice to insure good spice distribution.

3 Beat egg whites until stiff and reserve to fold in last. Beat egg yolks until light and reserve.

4 Combine molasses, sour milk, and egg yolks. Mix well. Add this mixture to sifted dry ingredients, blend in melted fat. Stir with as few strokes as possible. Carefully fold in stiffly beaten egg whites. Do not overmix. Batter will be lumpy.

5 Ladle batter onto preheated waffle baker. Bake 3 to 4 minutes until steaming stops.

6 Let waffle baker heat before pouring batter for next waffle.

waffles with unlimited fillings and toppings make excellent shortcakes

WAFFLE SHORTCAKES
4 servings

Choose as FILLING, TOPPING OR BOTH:

Sweetened strawberries
Sweetened cherries
Sliced bananas
Orange sections

Crushed pineapple
Sliced peaches
Whipped cream (optional)

WAFFLES:
8 Party Waffles (recipe on page 97)

1 ADVANCE PREPARATION: *Filling and Topping.* Prepare 2½ cups desired fruit or berries. Refrigerate.

2 Prepare waffles as directed.

3 Place 4 hot waffles on serving plates. Spoon about ½ cup fruit or berries on each. Cover with remaining waffles. Spoon the rest of fruit or berry mixture over top. Garnish with whipped cream if desired.

4 Serve immediately.

WAFFLE SUNDAE: 8 servings. Place hot waffles on serving plates. Use a scoop or so of ice cream and top with favorite dessert sauce, crushed fruit or sweetened berries.

an American version of French crêpe Suzette

FRENCH DESSERT CRÊPES

12 crêpes

1 cup sifted all-purpose flour	margarine
1½ tablespoons sugar	1 egg
¼ teaspoon salt	2 egg yolks
3 tablespoons melted butter or	1 cup milk

1   Turn dial to 3 or M and preheat griddle.
2   Sift together flour, sugar and salt into a mixing bowl.
3   Combine egg and egg yolks, beat lightly to blend. Reserve.
4   Blend butter into sifted dry ingredients. Gradually add milk and beat until smooth. Stir in beaten eggs. Beat mixture until bubbles appear on top.
5   Ladle 2 tablespoons batter for each pancake. Pour with a quick single motion. Bake 2 minutes or until pancake is bubbly and golden brown. Turn with a spatula and bake underside until golden brown.

ASSEMBLE: Place filling in each pancake. Roll carefully. Sprinkle with sugar if desired. Serve hot.

SUGGESTED FILLINGS

ORANGE. Place 1 tablespoon each of orange marmalade and heavy cream on each crêpe. Roll carefully.

JAM. Place 2 tablespoons jam on each crêpe. Roll.

DATES AND NUTS. Place mixture of 1 tablespoon finely chopped nuts, 1 tablespoon finely chopped dates and 1 teaspoon cream on each crêpe. Roll.

CANDIED FRUITS. Place 1 tablespoon each minced fruits and peels and chopped nuts on each crêpe. Roll.

STRAWBERRIES. Place 1 tablespoon sweetened cottage cheese on each crêpe. Roll. Top with sweetened strawberries.

a colorful dessert for special occasions

CHERRY DESSERT PANCAKES

4 servings

CHERRY SAUCE:
2 teaspoons cornstarch
2 tablespoons sugar
½ cup cherry juice
2½ cups frozen or canned, sweetened cherries, drained

DESSERT PANCAKES:
2 cups sifted all-purpose flour
3 tablespoons sugar
5 teaspoons baking power
½ teaspoon salt
2 eggs, separated
2½ cups milk
¼ cup melted butter or margarine

1 ADVANCE PREPARATION: *Cherry Sauce.* Combine constarch, sugar, and cherry juice, stir to blend. Cook over a low fire until thick. Add cherries and heat. Reserve. Heat just before serving.

2 Turn dial to 3 or M and preheat griddle.

3 Sift together flour, sugar, baking powder and salt into a mixing bowl.

4 Beat egg whites until stiff. Beat egg yolks until light. Add milk and mix well. Gradually add milk-egg mixture to sifted dry ingredients. Blend in melted butter. Carefully fold in beaten egg whites.

5 Test griddle. Ladle each pancake with a ¾ cup measure. Pour with a single, quick motion. Bake 2 minutes or until pancake is bubbly and golden brown. Turn to brown underside and bake 1 minute more.

6 *To serve:* Divide heated cherry sauce in half. Pour some in center of each pancake. Roll carefully. Garnish pancakes with remainder of cherry sauce.

our gratitude to Sweden for this unusual dessert

PLÄTTAR—SWEDISH DESSERT PANCAKES

16 2-inch pancakes

SPICED SAUCE:
¾ cup sugar
1½ tablespoons cornstarch
1 cup lingonberry juice
1 cup lingonberries
2 tablespoons lemon juice
¼ teaspoon allspice

DESSERT PANCAKES:
1½ cups sifted all-purpose flour
½ teaspoon cardamon
1 teaspoon salt
3 eggs
1 cup milk
3 tablespoons melted butter

1   ADVANCE PREPARATION: *Spiced Sauce.* Combine sugar and corn-starch. Add juice and cook until clear, stir constantly. Add lingonberries, lemon juice and allspice; blend well. Warm just before serving.

2   Tun dial to 3 or M and preheat griddle.

3   Sift together flour, cardamon and salt.

4   Beat eggs until light. Add milk and mix well. Gradually stir in sifted dry ingredients and melted butter. Stir only until well blended.

5   Test griddle. Ladle each pancake with 1 tablespoon measure. Pour with a single, quick motion. Bake 1 minute or until pancake is bubbly and golden brown. Turn to brown the underside and bake 1 minute more.

6   Serve the small pancakes with warm spiced sauce.

LINGONBERRIES may be purchased canned. Their lovely color and excellent flavor contribute to this attractive dessert pancake.

BLUEBERRY DESSERT PANCAKES. Use blueberries in the Spiced Sauce instead of lingonberries.

CRANBERRY DESSERT PANCAKES. Use cranberries in the Spiced Sauce instead of lingonberries.

a favorite mouth-watering dessert

MAPLE DESSERT WAFFLES

8 waffles

MAPLE TOPPING:
1 cup maple sugar or brown sugar
   with 3 drops maple flavoring
¼ cup water
¼ cup heavy cream

WAFFLES:
1 cup sifted cake flour
3 teaspoons baking powder
½ teaspoon salt
2 egg whites
2 eggs
1 cup heavy cream

1 ADVANCE PREPARATION: *Maple Topping.* Cook sugar and water until it is a thick syrup. Reserve and cool. Just before serving, whip heavy cream and fold into syrup.

2 Turn dial to 3 or M and preheat waffle baker.

3 Sift together flour, baking powder and salt into a mixing bowl.

4 Beat egg whites until stiff and reserve to fold in last. Beat whole eggs until light and blend in cream. Mix well.

5 Gradually add egg-cream mixture to sifted dry ingredients. Use as few strokes as possible. Carefully fold in stiffly beaten egg whites. Do not over mix. Batter will be lumpy.

6 Ladle batter onto preheated waffle baker. Bake 3 to 4 minutes until steaming stops.

7 Let waffle baker heat before pouring batter for next waffle.

8 Place maple topping on waffles. They may be served as single or double deckers as the appetite decides.

MAPLE DESSERT WAFFLES may also be prepared by topping plain waffles with ice cream and maple syrup. Chopped walnuts may be added as a garnish since the two flavors seem to be especially good together.

CONTINENTAL DESSERT PANCAKES
Serve hot

ALSATIAN. Use a favorite pancake recipe, add red currant or raspberry jelly to the batter.

AUSTRIAN. After pancakes are baked, use several fillings such as chocolate, soft cream cheese, jelly or jam. Stack these small pancakes with as many as three different fillings.

ENGLISH. Use a favorite pancake recipe and prepare 3-inch pancakes. Spread with butter and marmalade in layer cake style.

FRENCH. Use a favorite dessert pancake recipe for 3-inch pancakes. Place sweetened strawberries in the center of the pancake and roll. Top with powdered sugar and slivered almonds.

Use a favorite dessert pancake recipe for 3 inch pancakes. Fill the center with sweetened mashed bananas. Roll and sprinkle with powdered sugar.

NOTE:

Almost any jelly, jam, or sweetened berry or fruit filling can be used successfully in the rolled-up pancakes. Powdered sugar and slivered almonds are attractive.

a ski-resort dessert

ADIRONDACK PIE
6 *servings*

PANCAKES:
1 egg
1 cup milk
2 tablespoons melted fat
1 cup pancake quick-mix

FILLING:
Melted butter or margarine
Shaved maple sugar or brown
 sugar
Whipped cream

1 Turn dial to 3 or M and preheat griddle.

2 Beat egg until light. Add milk and fat. Mix well.

3 Gradually add egg-milk-fat mixture to pancake mix. Blend with a spoon just to moisten dry ingredients. Do not overmix. Batter will be lumpy.

4 Test griddle. Ladle each pancake with a ½ cup measure. Pour with a single, quick motion. Bake 2 minutes or until pancake is bubbly and golden brown. Turn with a spatula and bake 1 minute more.

5 Adirondack Pie is prepared by stacking the pancakes. Top each one with melted butter and maple sugar and the top one with whipped cream. Cut in pie shaped wedges and serve hot.

CRANBERRY JELLY instead of melted butter and maple sugar. Stack pancakes high. Top highest one with a sprinkling of confectioner's sugar or whipped cream.

index

127